a gift...

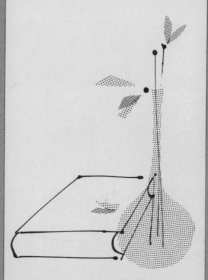

saint paul public library

from the publisher

the story of moslem art

Also by Christine Price

MADE IN THE MIDDLE AGES
MADE IN THE RENAISSANCE

Frontispiece:
A RULER GIVES AUDIENCE
*Miniature painting by Farhad for
the Khavaran-Nama. Persian, 1480
(The Metropolitan Museum of Art,
Rogers Fund, 1955)*

دلاور نبندد دل از مردِ جنگ
که ما را بد آید کسی کارِ نیست
زبان برکت در آن زبان حکمت
ابوالمحجن و سعدیل باکرم
بدیدند در که و میدانِ او
پیاده شد آن مرد و جنگ آزمای
برابر یکی تختِ زرین ببود
ابوالمحجن و سعد یکبار کام
اگر کرک باشد خدا و ندیج

که از سایهٔ خود در سهِ بلک
از این بیش تر جای کشتن نیست
که این و است ای خانه نیست
نهادند سر سوی بالای کوه
کیوان برآورده ایوانِ او
در ایوانِ شاهی نهاد و دید پای
نوادر بر آن تخت بنشسته بود
کشد دندلها بلفظِ سلام
یکمری ز یوسف ستاند خراج

شما را بد اندیشی اندر سر است
مغرب زمین مریم ابن زن
بیایید نزدیک شاهِ جهان
فرستاده ز پیش بسپرده را
همه رویِ ایوان گرفته بر
سرایی بد پدید آمد آسنه
همه خوشان از ابریشم هفت رنگ
سلامی که بهرِ سلامت بود
دو کرسی نهاد دند در پشگاه

نو اندیشه گر بدگشی دیگر است
نکتا باشته با بدِ کان
مدار ید از این سخنان نهان
بیا ورد ستان تا بدر که شاه
بطاق زبر جد رسانید سپر
درو چار صفه برافراخته
بپشش اندرون ابهای ملک
خرد را زبان جای ملامت بود
نشستند بهر دو نزد یکِ شاه

نوادر بگفتا ز بانِ دلب
بپرسید از زبانِ نیوب
از ای پدر بگرفت خاموش کنید
سخن آشکارا کنید از نهفت

the story of moslem art

BY CHRISTINE PRICE

Illustrated with photographs
and with drawings by the author

NEW YORK: E. P. DUTTON & CO., INC.

FIRST EDITION

contents

FOREWORD

IN TRYING TO span the centuries from the seventh to the twentieth, this book can only offer glimpses of the richness and variety of Moslem art, but I hope it will at least give an inkling of the wonders still to be explored in the architecture, the painting and the many arts and crafts of the Moslem world.

One or two points should perhaps be explained at the outset. To avoid confusion all dates are given according to the Western calendar rather than the Moslem one, which begins with the year 622 A.D., the date of Muhammad's flight from Mecca to Medina. Where an inscription is quoted, giving the Moslem date, the Western calendar year is indicated in brackets.

Throughout most of the book Iran is referred to as Persia, the name commonly used until the present day when the ancient name, Iran, has been revived. In the difficult task of transliterating Arabic, Persian and Turkish names I have been guided by the spelling used in *A Handbook of Muhammadan Art* by M. S. Dimand (The Metropolitan Museum of Art, New York, 1958), and in *Western Islamic Architecture* by John D. Hoag (Braziller, New York, 1963). Both books were indispensable references.

Above GUSHTASP AND THE BLACKSMITHS
Miniature from the Andarz Nama
Persian, 11th century (See page 56)

6

I am particularly indebted to Mr. Hoag and to Dr. Philip R. Adams, Director of the Cincinnati Art Museum, for their kindness in reading the manuscript and making valuable criticisms and suggestions. I am also most grateful to Professor K. A. C. Creswell for permitting me to use two of his photographs, one being taken from his book, *Early Muslim Architecture*, Vol. I (Clarendon Press, Oxford, 1932).

I am grateful to the Charles E. Tuttle Company, Rutland, Vermont, for permission to reproduce an illustration from *Turkish Miniature Painting* by Emel Esin; and to Thames and Hudson, London, for an illustration from *The Seljuks in Asia Minor* by Tamara Talbot-Rice.

The quotations on pages 94 and 95 are taken from *Clavijo's Embassy to Tamerlane*, 1403-1406, translated from the Spanish by Guy Le Strange (Broadway Travellers, London, and Harper & Row, Publishers, Inc., New York, 1928).

My grateful thanks are due to the following museums and libraries for permitting me to reproduce photographs of examples of Moslem art from their collections: the British Museum, London; the Cincinnati Art Museum, Cincinnati, Ohio; the Edinburgh University Library, Edinburgh, Scotland; The Metropolitan Museum of Art, New York; the Palestine Archaeological Museum, Jerusalem; the Pierpont Morgan Library, New York; the Victoria and Albert Museum, London; and the Worcester Art Museum, Worcester, Massachusetts.

I would also like to thank Miss Elizabeth Chase of the Yale University Art Gallery; Mr. Jackson W. Bird, Tehran; Mr. Alfred J. Hesler, Veedersburg, Indiana; and Mr. Lawrence Majewski, New York for the use of their photographs. Finally, I am deeply grateful to all those who gave help, encouragement and generous hospitality during my journey in the Near East, particularly to Mr. and Mrs. J. W. Bird in Tehran; to the Rev. and Mrs. Lewis Johnson and Dr. and Mrs. Robert Eaton in Meshed; and to Mr. J. P. Mulligan, the American Consul in Meshed.

C. P.

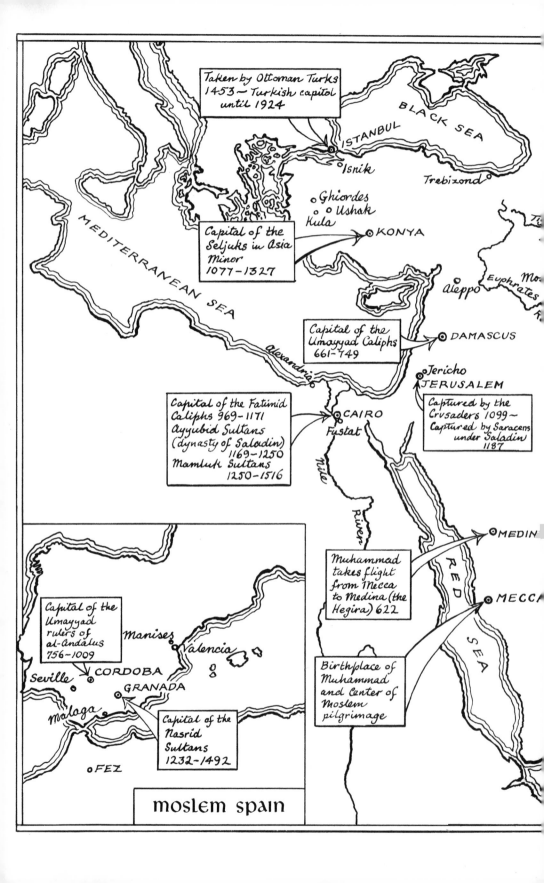

Taken by Ottoman Turks
1453 — Turkish capital
until 1924

BLACK SEA

ISTANBUL

Isnik

Trebizond

Ghiordes

Ushak

Kula

Capital of the
Seljuks in Asia
Minor
1077-1327

KONYA

Aleppo

Euphrates

MEDITERRANEAN SEA

Capital of the
Umayyad Caliphs
661-749

DAMASCUS

Alexandria

Jericho

JERUSALEM

Captured by the
Crusaders 1099 —
Captured by Saracens
under Saladin
1187

Capital of the Fatimid
Caliphs 969-1171
Ayyubid Sultans
(dynasty of Saladin)
1169-1250
Mamluk Sultans
1250-1516

CAIRO

Fustat

Nile

River

MEDIN

Muhammad
takes flight
from Mecca
to Medina (the
Hegira) 622

RED

MECCA

SEA

Capital of the
Umayyad
rulers of
al-Andalus
756-1009

Manises

Valencia

Seville

CORDOBA

GRANADA

Malaga

oFEZ

Capital of the
Nasrid
Sultans
1232-1492

Birthplace of
Muhammad
and center of
Moslem
pilgrimage

moslem spain

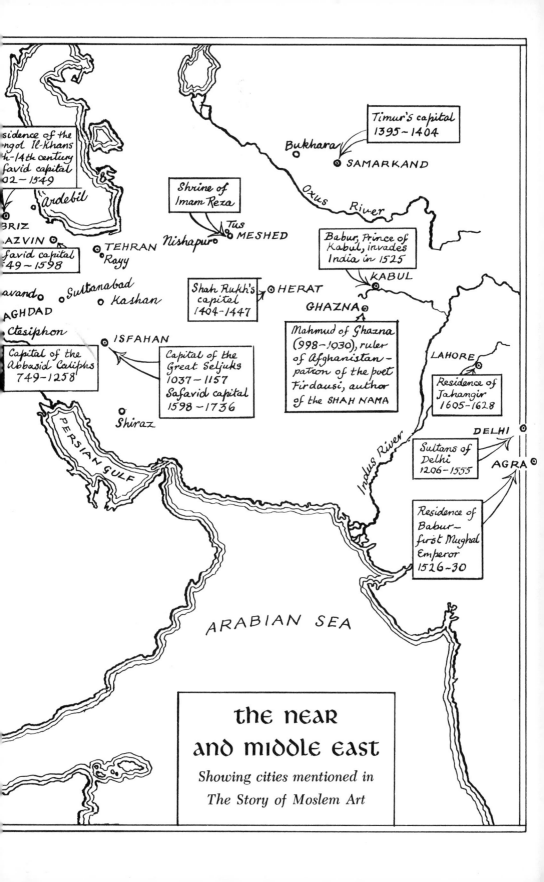

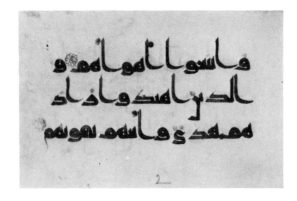

the BEGINNINGS of moslem ARt

THE STORY OF Moslem art begins with the clash of swords, the drumming of hoofs across the desert, and a mighty shout of triumph: *"Allahu akbar! God is most great!"*

This was the battlecry of the Arabs, thirteen centuries ago, when they burst over the borders of Arabia to conquer the world. They were united as brothers by Islam, the faith first preached by the Prophet Muhammad in the city of Mecca. They were waging a Holy War, as the Prophet had commanded them to do. Their faith in Allah, whose will controlled all things, made them fearless of death; and if they died in battle, would they not be carried at once to Paradise?

"There is no God but Allah, and Muhammad is his Prophet."

This was the faith that fired the Arabs when they swept northward into Syria in the year 633 and flung themselves against the might of the Byzantine Empire. The Emperor Heraclius, ruler of Syria, Egypt, and the whole eastern end of the Mediterranean, scorned the Arabs as mere desert raiders along the southern border of his vast domain. To the emperor and his heavily armed troops, the Syrian desert was an insuperable barrier; to the Arabs, on their swift camels and lean, hardy horses, it was a highway of conquest. They crossed the desert like a whirlwind, and fell upon the rich cities of Syria; by 636 they were masters of Damascus, Homs, Aleppo, and Antioch.

10

The Byzantine emperor discovered too late that the desert raiders were a power to be reckoned with, and he sent against them an army of fifty thousand. The Arabs were outnumbered two to one, but under the leadership of Khalid, "the sword of Allah," they crushed the Byzantines at the Battle of Yarmuk, near the river Jordan, on a terrible day of dust storms and fiery heat.

Then the Arabs swerved eastward to attack the ancient empire of Persia. Again the desert was their highway, leading them to the fertile valleys of the Tigris and Euphrates. The armies of the Persian emperor fled before them. The emperor deserted his fabulous palace at Ctesiphon by the Tigris, and left it to be looted by wild Arab tribesmen, many of whom had never seen gold before and could never have dreamed that such riches existed in all the earth.

While the conquerors of Ctesiphon fought on into the heart of Persia, another army of Arabs was cutting deeper into the Byzantine Empire in the west. They crossed the desert of Sinai and in 639 invaded Egypt and besieged the proud city of Alexandria. Within a year the city and all its treasures were theirs and they were pushing still farther westward along the North African coast.

In 642 the Arabs in the east scattered the Persian armies at the Battle of Nihavand, and the whole of Persia lay open to conquest. The desert towns of the interior surrendered, one by one, and soon the Arabs had crossed the Oxus River, on Persia's eastern boundary, and were swarming over the empty plains of Central Asia to conquer Bukhara and Samarkand. By the year 712 the spearhead of the Arab army had reached the border of India and occupied the lower valley of the Indus River.

Meanwhile Musa, the Arab governor of North Africa, had launched an attack on Spain. A raiding party of seven thousand, under a Berber named Tarik, took boats across the thirteen miles of sea between North Africa and Spain and landed near a mighty rock which they called Jebel Tarik—the Mount of Tarik—and which later became known as Gibraltar.

The Arabs routed the great army sent against them by the Visigothic King of Spain, and Tarik's raid became an invasion. City after city was seized by the Arabs, almost without a blow. Musa caught up with Tarik in Toledo and rebuked him for disobeying orders, but there was no stopping the conquest. Finally Musa himself was recalled from Spain by order of the caliph, the ruler of the Arab Empire, and he and Tarik returned triumphant to North Africa. They traveled eastward along the North African coast with a vast hoard of loot, and in their train of prisoners were four hundred Visigothic princes with crowns of gold. In the year 715 the victors arrived at the gates of Damascus in Syria and were welcomed in state by the Caliph al-Walid, successor of the Prophet Muhammad.

It was less than a century since Muhammad's death in 632, and the Arab Empire, united under the rule of the caliph, stretched from Spain to India. The Holy War had carried Islam to the ends of the earth. In the towns and cities of the empire, the cry of the *muezzin* rang out from the mosques, calling the Moslems to prayer and chanting the words of their belief: "There is no God but Allah, and Muhammad is his Prophet." Then, as now, the faithful prostrated themselves in prayer five times a day, in their homes, at their work, or in the mosque. Every year, throughout the month of Ramadan, they fasted from sunrise to sunset; they gave alms to the poor; and once in a lifetime, they made the pilgrimage to the holy city of Mecca in Arabia.

The laws they lived by were recorded in the Koran, the sacred book that contained the revelations Muhammad had received from heaven, through the Angel Gabriel. Arabic, the language of the Koran, had traveled far and wide with the conquerors and was soon to become the common tongue of the empire. It was a rich language, well suited to the poetry and speechmaking that the Arabs loved. Songs and stories took up no space in the saddlebags of the desert nomads and could be enjoyed night after night around the campfires. The art of the Arabs was in their speech, not in painting, sculpture, or building. Cities and towns were few in Arabia, and even among Arab merchants and towns-

BRONZE EWER
Persian, 5th–6th century

12

GILDED SILVER DISH
Persian, 5th century

HERO AND LION
*From a silk textile
Alexandria,
6th–7th century*

men there was no artistic tradition, apart from poetry and song.

The conquest revealed to the Arabs the wonders of craftsmanship and art. Nomads of the desert, who had always lived in black goat's-hair tents, suddenly found themselves rulers of great cities. They saw Greek and Roman temples, Persian palaces and Byzantine churches glittering with gold mosaics. They seized upon shining jewelry, metalwork and glassware, painted pottery, carved ivories, and silks of fantastic design. Their new settled life in towns brought the need for fine houses, richly furnished, and splendid mosques for the worship of Allah. The Arabs would have scorned to work as craftsmen themselves, but now, as masters of an empire, they could command the services of craftsmen and artists from Egypt, Syria, Greece, and Persia—countries with traditions of art going back for hundreds of years.

It was these conquered craftsmen, many of them never converted to Islam, whose arts were blended together under the rule of the Arabs to form what we know today as Moslem, or Islamic, art.

Down through the centuries many countries and many peoples have made their contributions to Moslem art, and to trace its story we must travel far in space as well as in time. We must sail the sea routes of the Mediterranean, the Red Sea, and the Indian Ocean, and we must march with the camel caravans of merchants and pilgrims from end to end of the Arab Empire.

We shall traverse some of the hottest countries in the world.

13

HORSEMAN
*From a silk
textile, Syrian
6th–7th century*

There will be low-lying coastal plains and river valleys, wide grassy steppes and ranges of snow-capped mountains; above all, our way will lead through lands of little rain, where sun blazes day after day in cloudless skies. Extending almost from Spain to India we shall find the great belt of desert country that was the highway of conquest for the invading tribesmen from Arabia. In North Africa and Egypt, Syria and Persia, we shall cross deserts of gravel and of shifting sand dunes, shaped by the wind; deserts white with salt and black with lava; barren lion-colored mountains and strange eroded hills where the naked soil is striped in red and green.

Our journeys will take us, like the travelers of long ago, to the cities of the Arab Empire, islands of civilization after the danger and loneliness of the road. There we shall visit mosques and palaces, the centers of Moslem art, and lose ourselves in the teeming lanes of bazaars where craftsmen work in little shops like caves, and merchants bring their wares from distant lands.

There is no better place to begin our travels than Damascus, the ancient caravan city chosen as the capital of the empire by the caliphs of the Umayyad clan. For centuries Damascus has been the goal and starting point of merchant caravans. Backed by the rampart of the Anti-Lebanon Mountains, the city faces east across the brown emptiness of the Syrian desert, and in the time of the early caliphs, the richest caravans came across the desert to the city's eastern gate. Their lean, weary camels were laden with silks and spices from Persia and Central Asia, and to the merchants and caravan leaders, worn out by weeks of desert travel, the green oasis of Damascus was the fairest sight in the world.

Orchards of figs, apricots, pomegranates, and nut trees still surround the city today, watered by the Barada River which rises in the mountains to the west. Though the days of camel caravans are gone, the bazaars of Damascus are thronged with merchants and craftsmen, and still standing in the center of the city is the Great Mosque where the Caliph al-Walid received in triumph the victors from Spain.

COURT AND SANCTUARY OF THE GREAT MOSQUE, DAMASCUS *(Photo: Creswell)*

Damascus and Syria

THE GREAT MOSQUE at Damascus was built on the site of a Roman temple of Jupiter. The Christians had a church there when the Arabs conquered Damascus in the seventh century, and for some years after the conquest, Moslems and Christians shared the same place of worship, entering the old temple area by two different doors. It was not until the year 705 that the Caliph al-Walid bought the church building and pulled it down in order to erect the mosque.

The first mosques in Arabia, in the time of Muhammad, were simple rectangular enclosures with one end roofed in as a protection against the weather. In the covered prayer hall there were no altars with statues of saints, vessels of gold and silver, and hangings of embroidery. Statues or pictures of living creatures were forbidden in the mosque. When Muhammad had converted the people of Mecca to Islam, he had smashed the pagan idols in the temple there. Only Allah could create human beings and

15

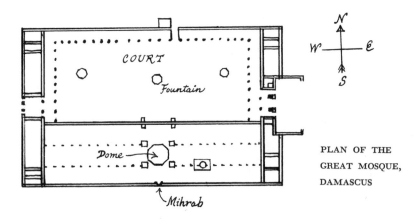

animals, and to have made pictures of Allah himself, as the Christians portrayed Christ, would have been unthinkable to a Moslem.

The furnishings of the mosque were as simple as the building. There was usually a pool in the courtyard where the worshipers washed before prayer. Entering the prayer hall barefooted, they knelt on carpets on the floor with their faces turned in the direction of Mecca. A pulpit called a *mimbar*, with steps leading up to it, was erected for the *imam*, or leader, who delivered the sermon and led the people in prayer on Friday, the Moslem holy day. The *imam* was not a priest in elaborate vestments. Any believer, from the caliph to the poorest man in the street, could mount the pulpit and preach to his brothers, for all men were equal before Allah.

The Great Mosque at Damascus was built according to the old rectangular plan, but on a grand scale; and the caliph gathered craftsmen from India, Persia, Egypt, and Constantinople to make it one of the most beautiful buildings in the world. The ancient temple enclosure formed the courtyard, large enough to be used by the caliph for audiences on ceremonial occasions. The old Roman towers at the corners were made into minarets from which the *muezzin* could send out the call to prayer far over the rooftops of the city. The courtyard was surrounded by arcades of columns and square piers. The lower parts of the walls were faced with paneling of colored marble, and above this were splendid mosaics.

16

VILLAGE ON A MOUNTAIN
*Detail of a mosaic
from the Great Mosque*

The making of pictures in mosaic, by setting tiny colored stones or cubes of glass in a surface of wet cement, was an ancient art of the Romans and Byzantines. Mosaics in churches included stately processions of saints and awe-inspiring visions of Christ in Majesty. In the mosque at Damascus, where figures were forbidden, the artists covered the walls with a magical landscape instead. We can still see and admire today the mountains and valleys, rivers and towns and little houses perched on rocky crags. In the words of an Arab traveler who visited the mosque in the thirteenth century, the mosaic portrays "all the cities of the world, and all its trees in green and gold and silver; its surface seems to drip gold and burn with flames."

The prayer hall on the south side of the courtyard was a large oblong building topped by a wooden dome. Rows of marble columns divided the interior into three aisles running across the building, to accommodate long lines of worshipers facing toward Mecca. The direction of Mecca was marked by an arched niche called the *mihrab* in the center of the back wall, an innovation that soon became general in mosques. The *mihrab* was gilded and aflame with precious stones; the capitals of the columns were also overlaid with gold, and the walls above them covered with mosaics that gleamed in the light of hundreds of hanging lamps.

The splendor of the mosque, built for the worship of Allah, was equaled by the palaces that the caliphs built for themselves. The days were past when caliphs lived as simply and austerely as their poorest followers. Muhammad had forbidden gambling, drinking wine, and wearing silken clothes, and had even frowned on music, but the Umayyad caliphs were too fond of art and pleasure to obey the Prophet's commands. They surrounded themselves with poets, musicians, and singers, and they dressed in silks and brocades with rich designs of animals, birds, and human figures. Yet they never forgot that they were men of the desert. They needed the freedom of wide, empty lands and the smell of clean air, and most of their time was spent in their desert palaces, far from the heat and bustle of Damascus.

The Caliph Hisham, who ruled from 724 to 743, built a palace in the bare, sun-bleached wilderness near Jericho. The site is barren and waterless today, but in Hisham's time an aqueduct brought water from the hills to the west. The palace was surrounded by a shady green park, and the name of the site, Khirbet al-Mafjar, means the place where water flows.

Trees and water were doubly precious to the Arabs, who had so often suffered from heat and thirst in the shadeless desert. In the Koran, Paradise is always described as a well-watered garden where the blessed may take their ease, and the word "paradise" comes from *pairidaeza,* an old Persian word meaning a park or an enclosed garden.

RUINS OF THE PALACE
Khirbet al-Mafjar

The Persians were famous for their gardens and palaces, and Persian builders and gardeners were probably employed at Khirbet al-Mafjar. The palace faced east across a courtyard with an ornamental pool in Persian style, and an archway in the façade opened into an inner court, surrounded by rooms. On the north side was the banqueting hall with a mosque behind it, and from the northwest corner a flight of steps and a passage led to the baths.

No palace was complete without an elaborate bath. The Arabs, like the Romans before them, considered personal cleanliness essential. In the Syrian cities they must have seen many old buildings left from the time of the Roman occupation, and the baths in the Arab palaces were on the Roman plan.

At Khirbet al-Mafjar the baths were lavishly decorated with carved stonework and even with statues, in defiance of the rule against portraying the human figure. The arched entrance, adorned with a statue of the caliph in a red-painted robe, led through a domed porch into a great hall, paved with mosaics. Down the south side of the hall was a swimming pool, and on the north side the small rooms of the bath and the furnace for heating. There were two hot rooms with hot air pipes under the marble floors and up the walls; two cold rooms for cooling off; a chamber with tanks for bathing; and a steam

19

CARVED STONEWORK
FROM THE PALACE

RECONSTRUCTED WINDOW
OF THE PALACE

PLASTER STATUE
OF THE CALIPH HISHAM

room in which steam came up through holes in the floor. Adjoining the bath was a small audience chamber for the caliph, paved with the finest of the mosaics—a pattern like a Persian carpet, and a semicircular design showing a tree with three gazelles and a lion, in black, bluish-green, and chestnut color.

The bath was the only part of Hisham's palace to be finished and in use when the building was wrecked by an earthquake in 748. The palace was never rebuilt, and a year after its destruction the Umayyad family was overthrown by their enemies the Abbasids, who were descendants of Muhammad's uncle, al-Abbas. After the first Abbasid caliph was established on the throne, one of his uncles, known as the Bloodshedder, invited the men of the Umayyad family to a feast, and slaughtered them. The only one to escape death was a young man named Abd er-Rahman, the grandson of Hisham. He fled westward to North Africa, and after five years of adventures, managed to find safety—and a kingdom for himself—in Spain.

The Abbasids had been supported by the Persians, and having seized command of the empire, they moved the capital eastward, nearer to Persia. The Abbasid Caliph al-Mansur chose a site on the bank of the Tigris, which loops and twists through the desert like a sluggish brown snake, and within four years a hundred thousand workers had built there the glorious city of Baghdad.

MOSAIC IN AUDIENCE
CHAMBER OF THE BATH
Khirbet al-Mafjar

LUSTER-PAINTED BOWL
WITH INSCRIPTION:
"BLESSING"
Mesopotamian,
10th century

the splendor of baghdad

BAGHDAD WAS built as a round city, encircled by a moat and two mighty brick walls. In the center, surrounded by a third wall, rose the green-domed palace where the caliph lived in remote magnificence, like the Persian emperors of old.

Persians helped to build the city and to fill the houses with beautiful things. The Arabs in Baghdad soon adopted Persian dress and food, and drank their wine from cups and bowls of Persian pottery. Muhammad had said that "he who drinks from gold and silver vessels drinks the fires of hell." Gold and silver were reserved for the blessed in Paradise, and everyone else should be content with brass, copper, and clay. The craftsmen of Baghdad worked hard to make these everyday materials as lovely as precious metal. Bronze vessels were inlaid with copper, and the simple shapes of pottery were enriched with painted designs. The potters also discovered how to paint their wares with "gold luster," a mixture of silver and copper oxides that gave the pottery a golden gleam.

But no imitation of gold would satisfy Harun ar Rashid, the caliph made famous in the *Arabian Nights.* At the feasts in his palace the roasts of duck, turkey, and suckling lamb, laid in beds of saffron rice, were served on dishes of gold and jewels. The carpets on the floor were studded with gems, and the guests of honor showered with pearls.

21

EARTHENWARE EWER
Persian, 9th century

In the reign of Harun ar Rashid, at the end of the eighth century, envoys came to Baghdad from the Kingdom of the Franks. They were two Frankish nobles, Sigismund and Lentfrid, with a Jewish interpreter, Isaac, and they brought gifts for the caliph from Charlemagne. The two Franks must have been dazzled by the wealth of the city and the caliph's court. Their own country and most of Europe were still struggling through the Dark Ages, the turbulent period of wars and barbarian invasions that followed the fall of the Roman Empire. Charlemagne encouraged education and scholarship in his dominions, but he himself, a warrior from boyhood, was hardly able to write his own name.

The envoys found the caliph and his nobles men of high culture and learning. The palace was a meeting place for scholars and scientists from many lands. They were translating into Arabic the scientific works of Persian, Syrian, and Indian authors, and the caliph's own physician made Arabic versions of the ancient Greek classics of medicine by Hippocrates and Galen. Skilled artists and craftsmen were employed at the court to make books of the new translations and magnificent copies of the Koran. Paper was manufactured for the pages—a secret learned from the Chinese—and the texts were written out in the angular Kufic script, the early form of Arabic writing.

Students of physics at the caliph's court delighted in ingenious mechanical inventions, and among the gifts the caliph sent to Charlemagne was an astonishing water clock. Tradition says he also sent silks, Eastern spices, a carved ivory chess set, and an elephant named Abu'l Abbas, the first elephant ever seen in the land of the Franks. Abu created a sensation among Charlemagne's people, and was deeply mourned at his death in 810. A carved ivory elephant, supposed to come from the caliph's chess set, has survived to this day. Chess, as yet unknown in the West, had come to Baghdad from Persia, and was a popular game at court. The elephant is the piece that in Western Europe is called the bishop.

Craftsmen who could make such things as the caliph's chess set were important people in Baghdad. The wealth of the city

DESIGN OF SILK TEXTILE
Persian, 8th–9th century

22

EARTHENWARE BOWL
Mesopotamian,
9th century

CARVED IVORY
CHESSMAN
Mesopotamian

depended on its craftsmen and merchants. Most crafts and trades had separate streets of their own, and the shops of Baghdad displayed goods from all parts of the known world. Here were carpets from Spain and leatherwork from North Africa; glassware of Syria and fine Egyptian textiles; swords from Damascus, and furs and earthen jars of honey from the cold lands of the north.

Caravans of camels, laden with merchandise, came daily to the city along the four great roads that led to the four corners of the empire and converged at the caliph's palace. The products of neighboring lands were brought down the Tigris to Baghdad on rafts and river boats, and the docks of the city were crowded with shipping and loud with the babel of voices in a score of tongues. On the waterfront were Arab sea captains, like Sindbad the Sailor, whose ships had docked downstream at the port of Basra, or at Siraf on the Persian Gulf. They were newly returned from India with a fortune in spices and jewels, or from China with silks and gauzes and delicate cream-colored porcelain.

There was a constant coming and going of Arab travelers by sea and land. Everywhere they went in the Arab Empire Moslems could be sure of a welcome among people speaking Arabic, worshiping in the mosque and living by the laws of the Koran. Pilgrims journeyed to Mecca; scholars visited famous schools;

23

and even craftsmen traveled far and wide, wherever their skill was needed.

Roads and sea routes were highways for ideas as well as for merchandise. Seeing the work of their fellows in distant cities, the craftsmen learned new skills and new schemes of decoration. Styles of art were soon so mixed together that Syrian silkweavers in Damascus borrowed ideas from the Persians, and designs used by the sculptors of Baghdad were echoed in the work of ivory carvers in Spain.

Baghdad and Córdoba, the capital of Moslem Spain, were separated by hundreds of miles of land and sea but closely linked together by their rivalry. The Arabs of Spain wanted their capital to be the equal of Baghdad in wealth and art and learning. Their country was growing rich and prosperous under the successors of Abd er-Rahman, the last of the Umayyads, who had gained control of Spain after his flight from Damascus.

The Umayyad rulers of Spain had no cause for friendship with the Abbasid caliphs of Baghdad, and in the tenth century, when the power of the caliphs was waning, Abd er-Rahman III declared his independence from Baghdad, and set himself up as caliph in Spain. It was in his reign that Córdoba reached the height of its glory and became the goal of merchants, pilgrims, scholars, and artists from all over the empire.

"Do not talk of the Court of Baghdad and its glittering magnificence," wrote one of the poets of Moslem Spain; "do not praise Persia and China and their manifold advantages; For there is no spot on earth like Córdoba. . . ."

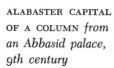

ALABASTER CAPITAL OF A COLUMN *from an Abbasid palace, 9th century*

córdoba, capital of al-andalus

THE PRIDE OF Córdoba was its Great Mosque, one of the largest of all mosques, and the holiest shrine of Western Islam. Moslem pilgrims from far and near took the highway to Córdoba through the rolling green countryside of Andalusia, known to its Arab rulers as al-Andalus. The city lay on the north bank of the Guadalquivir; it was girdled by a high wall, but houses, gardens, and orchards had spilled beyond the wall and spread along both sides of the river valley.

The tall minaret of the mosque rose like a beacon for tired pilgrims, trudging over the long Roman bridge that spanned the river. A short steep street led up from the bridge and skirted the western wall of the mosque. The pilgrims turned aside through an archway in the wall, and as they entered the courtyard in front of the prayer hall, the weariness of the journey was forgotten and they were in another world.

All was peace and quietness. They could see far into the interior of the prayer hall through the open arches along the north end of the building. Lines of orange trees spread cool shade in the court, and the rows of slender tree trunks were continued within the building by rows of marble columns that faded away into the distance toward the *mihrab*.

COURT OF THE
MOSQUE OF CÓRDOBA

The Great Mosque is now a cathedral, but even today, as you enter the building from the orange-tree court, it is difficult to think of it as a Christian church. The ancient prayer hall is so vast that the cathedral choir and sanctuary, erected in the heart of the building in the sixteenth century, are lost in the dim forest of columns. The building is darker than it used to be when the Moslem pilgrims came there to pray. The open archways facing the court have been closed, and the many glass lamps that used to hang from the ceiling are gone.

Just inside the entrance, you walk through aisles of columns built in the eighth century, when work on the mosque was begun by the first Abd er-Rahman, the fugitive from Damascus. The smooth marble pillars, taken from old Roman buildings, were not tall enough to support the roof. The Arab builders devised an ingenious system of double arches to increase the height, and with their love of color, they built the arches of red brick and cream-colored stone in alternating stripes.

Walking southward, you pass through aisles built by Abd er-Rahman II to make room for growing crowds of worshipers. Then the arches become more richly decorated, and between them you

THE MOSQUE OF CÓRDOBA:
ARCADES BUILT BY
ABD ER-RAHMAN I

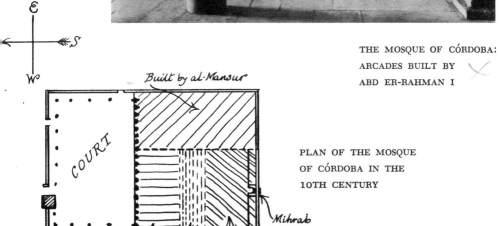

E

S

W

Built by al-Mansur

COURT

Mihrab

PLAN OF THE MOSQUE
OF CÓRDOBA IN THE
10TH CENTURY

Built by Abd er-Rahman I   Built by   Built by Hakam II
                           Abd er-Rahman II

ARCHES IN FRONT
OF THE MIHRAB
LOOKING WEST
(Mihrab on the lef♦

can see the *mihrab*, a deep recess in the south wall, surrounded by glittering gold mosaics. The arches in front of the *mihrab* are fantastically interlaced, and the vaults above form three exquisite small cupolas over the aisle along the south wall.

This beautiful southern end of the building was the work of craftsmen employed by Hakam II, the gentle and scholarly caliph who ruled in Córdoba in the late tenth century. His artists adorned the *mihrab*, the vaults, and the arches with panels of plaster and white marble carved in relief with complicated designs of twining stems, flowers and leaves—the type of design that became known as arabesque and that we shall meet in endless variety in all branches of Moslem art.

28

VAULT OVER THE
CENTRAL BAY IN
FRONT OF THE MIHRAB

The lovely floral arabesques in mosaic around the arch of the *mihrab* were the work of a craftsman from Constantinople, sent to Córdoba by the Byzantine emperor at Hakam's special request.

The arch on the right of the *mihrab*, also decorated with mosaic, was the caliph's private entrance to the mosque, reached by a covered passage from his riverside palace, the Alcazar. The left-hand arch opened into rooms where treasures were kept. The greatest treasure of the mosque was a large copy of the Koran that contained four pages written by the hand of Uthman, one of the earliest caliphs of the Arab Empire and a companion of the Prophet Muhammad. Uthman was murdered, and the pages were stained with his blood. This precious book was brought out only for the Friday service, and every pilgrim to Córdoba longed to see it, as the crowning glory of his pilgrimage.

29

DETAIL OF MOSAIC
ABOVE THE ARCH
OF THE MIHRAB

Some of the artists who worked so brilliantly for Hakam II in the mosque also decorated the new palace-city of Medina az-Zahra for his father, Abd er-Rahman III. Medina az-Zahra, the Palace of the Flower, was laid out on a hillside four miles northwest of Córdoba. It required thirteen years to build, and Abd er-Rahman, with his government officials and huge household, moved into the new palace a few years before his death in 961.

Today Medina az-Zahra is in ruins, with many of the buildings buried under the grass of the surrounding fields. The palace-city was built on three broad terraces on the slope of the hill, backed by the low range of the Sierra Morena, and looking out over the river valley to the walls and towers of Córdoba. Only parts of the two upper terraces have been excavated. The main entrance in the encircling wall was on the north side, where a ramp wide enough for horsemen led down through two great doorways. To the right, on the top terrace, were houses and courtyards, kitchens and bakeries, and to the left, a large pillared hall facing a patio garden. Beyond the garden another ramp descended to the level of the second terrace where there was a bath with a number of small rooms, and west of the bath, an audience chamber overlooking a big rectangular pool.

This splendid building, which consisted of a central throne room with two flanking halls, has been restored and roofed over. Marble columns and horseshoe-shaped arches have been set up, and thousands of fragments of carved stonework that formerly covered the walls are being fitted into place again. One of the windows has a white marble frame carved at the top in the form of a beautiful scallop shell. The marble jamb of a doorway is covered with floral arabesques in relief, and in the petals of the sculptured flowers are tiny holes, originally set with gems.

On great occasions, when the caliph received ambassadors at the palace, the doors and archways of his throne room were draped in silk and the pink marble floor was richly carpeted. Large square niches in the walls held vases of flowers or metal incense burners from which the aromatic smoke drifted out to perfume the air. Many lamps hung from the beams of the ceiling,

CARVED STONEWORK
FROM MEDINA AZ-ZAHRA

and the whole room must have glowed like a jewel, reflected in the still water of the pool.

Foreign ambassadors were met at the palace gate by officials clad in silk and brocade, and the way to the audience chamber was spread with carpets. Arab chroniclers tell us that the caliph sat on a throne of gold and gems, surrounded by his sons and the chief dignitaries and wise men of the kingdom. One of his audience chambers was said to be entirely sheathed in gold, and shone with a blinding brightness. A huge pearl was set in the ceiling, and in the floor was a pool of mercury. When the mercury was stirred, at the caliph's command, strange lights quivered over the gleaming walls until the whole room seemed to be slowly revolving.

After their awesome reception by the caliph, foreign envoys were usually presented with robes of silk and cloth of gold. These were adorned with bands, called *tiraz*, with the caliph's name in Kufic script either embroidered or woven into the material. There was a special *tiraz* factory at the palace for producing these robes, which were also given as rewards to ministers of state.

Among other beautiful and costly gifts, made by the craftsmen of the palace, were small ivory boxes, used for holding perfumes and frequently carved with an inscription, telling the name of the owner. The box on page 25, made for the daughter of Abd er-Rahman III, is adorned with deeply cut arabesques that remind us of the decorations of the mosque and palace.

Another ivory box, even more elaborate, bears the inscription "(The blessing of Allah) and prosperity and good fortune to Ziyad ibn Aflah, Prefect of Police. Made in the year 359 (969–970)." Ziyad was the son of a slave of Abd er-Rahman III, and rose to a position of power as Prefect of Córdoba in the reign of Hakam. Three scenes around Ziyad's box depict him seated on a throne, riding on horseback with a falcon on his fist, and mounted in state upon an elephant. A wealth of carved animals fill the spaces between the scenes. Beside hounds chasing hares, there are winged griffins, fantastic beasts that can also be seen on the

patterned silk textiles of the time. Camels, elephants, and pea-cocks are among the varied creatures carved on an ivory box made in the early eleventh century. Two scenes on the front show people eating and drinking and playing musical instruments. One musician plays a kind of oboe called a *zamr*, and another an *'oud*, the short-necked lute that originated in Persia and was passed on by the Arabs to Western Europe in the Middle Ages.

The artists of the palace even produced sculpture in the round. This little bronze deer formed part of a fountain, with water pouring from its open mouth. The sculptor had no interest in making a naturalistic animal. The contours are smoothed out and simplified, and the whole body is covered with arabesques. Animals and birds also appear on the painted pottery found during the excavations of Medina az-Zahra, some of it probably imported from Baghdad. Pottery bowls, like the ivory boxes, were often inscribed with such mottoes as "Blessing and ease to the owners."

Those who lived at Medina az-Zahra may have enjoyed ease and blessing for a while, but not for long. Hakam II was a man of middle age when he came to the throne, and his reign was short.

PEACOCK
*Painted on a
pottery bowl,
Medina az-Zahra*

BRONZE DEER
FROM A FOUNTAIN
*Medina az-Zahra,
10th century*

After his death, the power was usurped by his minister, al-Mansur, who was acting as regent for the caliph's young son. Al-Mansur built a new palace on the other side of Córdoba, and moved into it with the government in 981. He waged war against the Christians in the north of Spain, pushing deep into Christian territory. He also enlarged the Great Mosque, extending the prayer hall and courtyard to the east, but he had little time or money to spend on art, and his addition to the building was an inferior imitation of the earlier work.

Soon after the death of al-Mansur in 1002, the government of Córdoba collapsed and civil war broke out. Berber mercenary soldiers from North Africa sacked and destroyed al-Mansur's palace and broke into Medina az-Zahra and stripped it of its treasures. After twenty years of anarchy, the proud kingdom of al-Andalus was broken up. The Spanish caliphate was abolished, and Córdoba became one city among many independent cities, each ruled by a petty Moslem prince.

POTTERY
FROM
MEDINA
AZ-ZAHRA

While Córdoba was torn by civil war and looted by barbarians, another city of the Arab Empire had risen to greatness and another provincial ruler had declared himself to be an independent caliph. The new city of Cairo in Egypt, founded by the Fatimid dynasty in the tenth century, had become a center of art to rank with Baghdad and Córdoba in the days of their splendor.

RUINS OF MEDINA AZ-ZAHRA
FROM THE NORTHWEST

cairo and the fatimid caliphs

BY THE MIDDLE of the eleventh century Cairo was "a great town to which few cities can be compared."

This was the opinion of a Persian traveler who passed through Egypt on a pilgrimage to Mecca. He visited Cairo during the reign of al-Mustansir, the richest of the Fatimid caliphs, a young man of scholarly tastes whose vast library included hundreds of beautifully decorated copies of the Koran. The forebears of Mustansir, who traced their descent from Fatima, the daughter of the Prophet Muhammad, had invaded Egypt in the year 969 from their base in Tunis. Having seized control of the country and established Cairo as their capital, they went on to conquer Palestine and Syria and to become masters of Jerusalem, the holy city of Christians, Moslems, and Jews.

The wealth of the Fatimid Empire poured into Cairo where the caliphs kept huge storehouses of treasures and works of art. Egypt had had a number of different capital cities since the ancient times of the Pharaohs, but all were close to the Nile, the great river that brought life to the rainless Egyptian desert, watering the irrigated farmlands and spreading them with fresh rich soil at the season of flood.

The Arab conquerors of Egypt in the seventh century had

founded their capital on the east bank of the Nile near the beginning of the vast delta, where the waters of the river wandered over the flat land through many twisting channels. The Arab city was called Fustat, the Town of the Tent. Two royal suburbs were added to Fustat by rulers of Egypt in the eighth and ninth centuries, but the old Town of the Tent remained the center of trade, commerce, and crafts, even after the building of the new Fatimid capital.

Cairo, the city of the Fatimid caliphs, lay northeast of Fustat and about a mile from the bank of the Nile, on the old north-south caravan road to the Red Sea. Protected by a wall with eight gateways, Cairo was designed as a palace-city and seat of government, like Medina az-Zahra. The palace of the caliphs stood in the center, overlooking a broad parade ground for troops, and close by was the great mosque al-Azhar, which became, and has remained ever since, a famous school of Moslem religious teaching.

Nothing remains of the Fatimid palace today except some roof-beams carved with scenes of life in the court and countryside. Here we see hunters and falconers, musicians with flute and 'oud, and desert travelers like the Persian pilgrim, journeying on foot or in curtained litters on the backs of camels. Eager as any tourist of today to see all he could, the Persian managed to gain access to the palace, and tells us that it consisted of twelve square pavilions, each more beautiful than the last. In the final pavilion, which was carpeted and draped in Greek satin, stood a huge golden throne decorated with hunting scenes. The tables, set for a feast, were adorned with astonishing sculptures in sugar, one of them in the form of an orange tree, complete with branches, leaves, and fruit.

MUSICIANS AND TRAVELING MERCHANTS
Wood carvings from the Fatimid Palace

CARVED WOOD PANEL
Egyptian, 11th century

ROCK CRYSTAL EWER
Egyptian, 10th–11th century

The rich people of Cairo lived in great luxury. Their fine houses, built around the palace-city of the caliph, were mostly five or six stories high, and were set in gardens where trees bore fruit the whole year round. In Fustat was a house of seven stories that actually had a roof garden, where a bullock was put out to graze among fruit trees and sweet-smelling flowers.

But by far the most extraordinary sight in Fustat was the bazaar, called the Market of the Lamps. Rare and precious objects could be found there from all parts of the world. There were boxes, combs, and sheaths for knives, made of mother-of-pearl; and beautiful vessels, large and small, carved from rock crystal, with designs of arabesques, animals and birds. There were ivory tusks from African elephants, and even the spotted skins of giraffes, which were made into slippers.

The craftsmen of Fustat made all kinds of pottery, some of it so thin it was almost transparent. Many of the bowls, cups, and plates were painted in shining gold luster that changed color, like shot silk, in changing light. The secret of making gold-luster pottery was probably brought to Egypt by potters from Baghdad where lusterware had been made in the time of Harun ar Rashid.

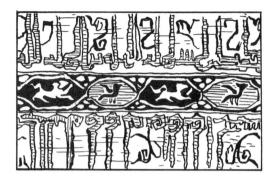

LINEN CLOTH WITH
WOVEN INSCRIPTION
WITH THE NAME OF
THE FATIMID CALIPH
AZ-ZAHIR (1021–36)

But while the Baghdad potters generally used abstract patterns, the Egyptians preferred designs of animals and people.

In the wonderful bazaar the Persian traveler also found vessels of green glass, clear and brilliant as emeralds; white glassware with enameled decorations; and tall copper vases from Damascus which "shine so brightly one takes them for gold." Egyptian weavers were famous for their skill, and the traveler must have seen at Fustat the fine linen textiles that were woven there. Some of the linens had elaborate printed patterns in several colors, stamped on the cloth with woodblocks. Then there were shot silks used for sumptuous saddlecloths and the curtains of camel litters, and silks, linens, and woolens with woven or embroidered designs sparkling with threads of gold. The most beautiful stuffs of all—not for sale in the bazaar—were the products of the royal *tiraz* factories, reserved for the use of the caliph and bearing his name in Kufic letters between bands of decoration.

Of all the wonderful things made in Egypt in the time of the Fatimid caliphs, few have survived until today. Soon after the Persian pilgrim traveled on toward Mecca by the road to the Red Sea, Egypt was embroiled in a civil war. The Turkish troops in the palace revolted and sacked the caliph's treasury. Vases of crystal and gold, sculptures of birds and beasts and trees in gold and jewels, armor and vessels of inlaid metal, enormous tents of silk and brocade with tentpoles of silver—all were scattered as loot, and the Turks ripped the leather covers from the priceless books to make shoes for their slaves.

LION DESIGN *From a block-printed linen*
Egyptian, 10th century

38

The Fatimid caliphs, like the caliph in Baghdad, were losing their power, and their wide possessions were shrinking, year by year. By the middle of the eleventh century the Seljuk Turks from Central Asia, who had already penetrated the Arab lands in great numbers as mercenary soldiers, had launched a full-scale invasion of the Arab Empire. The Turks were nomads who lived on horseback; they were experts at lightning attack; and as converts to Islam they had a fanatical zeal for their new faith.

Sweeping across Persia from the steppes of Turkestan, the Seljuks came to Baghdad in 1055 and took command of the city under their leader, Tughril Beg, who formally swore loyalty and obedience to the helpless Abbasid caliph. The following year Tughril Beg was appointed sultan by the caliph and called "King of the East and West." After the death of the Turkish leader, his nephew Alp Arslan, the Lion, pressed on toward Syria and the West. In 1071 Turkish forces defeated the army of the Byzantine emperor and conquered the greater part of Asia Minor. In the same year they drove the Egyptians out of Palestine and captured the holy city of Jerusalem.

A great outcry arose in Western Europe at the fall of Jerusalem. Under the Fatimid rulers the city had usually been open to Christians; the fanatical Turks forbade the entry of pilgrims to visit the Christian Holy Places. In 1096, at the summons of the Pope and the preaching of Peter the Hermit, the nobles, knights, and commoners of Europe took up arms and vowed to rescue the Holy City from the infidel. A mighty army put on the badge of the Cross and rolled slowly eastward, thirsting for the blood of the Saracens, the men of the East.

This was the First Crusade, and the first time in history that Christians of Western Europe—not a mere trickle of pilgrims but an army of many thousands—had invaded the Arab Empire, confronted the Moslems on their own home ground, and seen for themselves some of the wonders of Eastern civilization.

Left WOVEN DESIGN FROM LINEN TEXTILE *Egyptian, 11th century*

Within image, scroll at top reads (in medieval Latin script):

> hec est dispositio et figura templi domini sepulchri superna

Within image, bottom banner reads:

> Intra templu sepulchri domini locatus est lapis iste super quo christus cruci baiulus ori dum...

JERUSALEM AND THE CRUSADERS

ON THURSDAY, July 14, 1099, the Crusaders launched their attack on Jerusalem. The walled city crowning its rocky hill seemed almost impregnable. The great gates were closed and the walls lined with defenders. For many days, enduring tortures of thirst and heat, the army of the attackers had been encamped about the city. They had built tall siege towers and set up battering rams and catapults, and they had marched barefooted in solemn procession, carrying figures of saints and singing psalms. Now at last the siege towers were moved up close to the walls; the huge battering rams swung into action, and the catapults began to bombard the walls with stones.

While the defenders hurled down rocks and boiling oil, the bombardment went on all day and all the next day until mid-afternoon. Then the Crusaders saw a vision of St. George, urging them on to victory. They let down the drawbridge from one of the siege towers to the top of the city wall, and the attackers charged across the bridge and swarmed into the city. They rushed down the narrow streets, killing men, women, and children. The defense collapsed; Jerusalem was conquered.

40

Only the fall of Mecca itself could have been a greater tragedy to the Moslems than the loss of Jerusalem. Ever since the conquest of the city by the Arabs in the seventh century, Jerusalem had been a place of pilgrimage for Moslems. Within the eastern wall of the city, where the Jewish Temple had stood in the time of Christ, was one of the holiest places of Islam, known as the Haram, or Sanctuary. From here Muhammad made a miraculous ascent into heaven, and in the center of the Haram was the sacred Rock where Abraham prepared for the sacrifice of Isaac.

In the year 688 the Caliph Abd al-Malik decided to build over the Rock a splendid dome that would rival the dome of the Church of the Holy Sepulcher. He sent letters throughout the Arab Empire with an appeal for money and for skilled craftsmen, and as the funds were collected, a small domed building was erected beside the Rock to serve as a treasury. This became the model for the Dome of the Rock itself. The beautiful Dome was not intended to be a mosque but a shrine in which worshipers paced around the Rock while they said their prayers. A congregational mosque, large enough for hundreds of worshipers, was built on the south side of the Haram and was called al-Aqsa, The Remote, because of its distance from Mecca.

On the day of the Crusaders' victory the white pavement of the Haram was red with blood and strewn with the sprawling heaps of the dead. The Moslem population of the city was almost exterminated. Yet in spite of their hatred of the Moslems, the Crusaders must have gazed in wonder at the Dome of the Rock. They had never seen a building to match it. The eight-sided walls and the dome itself were covered with mosaics, and the whole building sparkled in the sunshine like a casket set with jewels.

CRUSADER AND SARACEN
*From a 14th-century
English manuscript*

Inside, the rough surface of the Rock rose in the center of the floor, surrounded by a double arcade of columns and piers with gilded capitals.

Instead of destroying the building, the Crusaders turned it into a church. They crowned the dome with a golden cross, built an altar on the Rock, and set up holy pictures and statues of saints. They even erected an iron grille around the Rock to protect it from the Christian pilgrims who broke off pieces to carry away as relics. The Crusaders were so impressed by the Dome that the same circular plan was used for churches in Europe, particularly those associated with the Knights Templars, such as the round Temple Church in London.

The Templars were an order of knights dedicated to the protection of Christian pilgrims, and during the Crusaders' occupation

THE DOME OF THE ROCK
AND THE TEMPLE AREA
(*Mosque of al-Aqsa in the background at the right*)

of Jerusalem they had their quarters in the Mosque of al-Aqsa. A flight of steps led down from the Dome of the Rock to the open courtyard in front of the mosque. Al-Aqsa had been badly damaged by earthquakes and entirely rebuilt by one of the Fatimid caliphs in 1035, but the original plan was still preserved. With its aisles running north and south, the building was similar to the mosque at Córdoba, but the aisles were wide, the ceiling lofty, and the whole effect of the interior more open. The Templars used part of the mosque as a church and part as living quarters, but they allowed Moslems to come and pray there. It was only the newly arrived knights, unused to the ways of the East, who objected to the presence of Moslems in the mosque, praying with their faces toward Mecca.

43

SARACEN WARRIOR
Detail of inlaid
decoration of
brass writing box
on page 56

Crusaders who stayed long in Syria and Palestine grew to be tolerant of their enemies. During lulls in the fighting, Christians and Moslems lived quietly side by side. Pilgrims passed unmolested to Jerusalem and to Mecca, and Christian knights and Moslem nobles sallied forth from their castles, not to wage war but to hunt over each other's land with hawk and hound. The Crusaders began to realize how much they could learn from the Saracens, the men of the East. They had come to Palestine convinced of their own superiority, expecting to find themselves fighting against ignorant heathens. Instead they found people of culture and refinement who despised the men of the West—the Franks, they called them—as crude, dirty, and superstitious.

The Saracens were highly skilled in war. The proud warriors, mounted on their swift horses, wore shirts of chain mail, woven of many tiny steel links. Their swords were the finest Damascus blades, and on each man's shield was a painted device by which he was known—an idea that was copied by the Crusaders and developed into the art of heraldry. When the Saracens rode in battle array with silken banners flying, each leader had his military band of drums, trumpets, and woodwinds. The Crusaders, who

44

used only horns and trumpets, must have been thrilled by the martial rhythm of the drums. The cylindrical drum, or *tabl*, and the kettledrum, called *naqqara* by the Arabs, were soon introduced into Europe, where they were known as the tabor and the naker. There were even new ideas in military architecture to be learned from the Saracens, when the Crusaders began to build castles in Palestine and Syria; but what impressed the Europeans most of all were the wonderful arts and crafts of their enemies, and the luxury of their life.

In the warm climate of the Near East, where gardens were filled with unimaginable fruits and flowers, men and women dressed in soft silken stuffs instead of heavy woolens, and feasted on foods flavored with exotic spices and sweetened with sugar. The Christian rulers of Jerusalem and of the Crusader States on the Syrian coast soon adopted Eastern dress and habits and chose to live in houses like Arab palaces, equipped with elaborate baths, unknown in the cold gloomy castles of the north. Instead of spreading their floors with rushes or straw and sitting on hard oaken chairs, they stepped barefooted on colorful carpets and lounged on divans with silken cushions. Their rooms were furnished with low tables of wood inlaid with mother-of-pearl, and bronze incense burners patterned with arabesques, and they sipped their wine from goblets of delicate Syrian glass.

Many Crusaders preferred to stay in the East, and those who returned home carried with them treasures of Moslem art. Eastern silks, so rare and precious in Europe, were presented to churches, and textiles with Arabic inscriptions were made into church

TEXTILE DESIGNS
OF EAST AND WEST:
Left GERMAN
BLOCK-PRINTED LINEN
13th–14th century
Right PERSIAN SILK
11th–12th century

vestments or used as wrappings for holy relics. Brass ewers, bowls, and incense burners, gold-luster pottery and Syrian glass also found their way into the treasuries of churches and castles. The shapes and inlaid patterns of Near Eastern metalwork gave fresh inspiration to the craftsmen of Europe, while Italian weavers and German cloth printers copied the strange animal and bird designs of the Eastern fabrics.

Enterprising merchants followed in the wake of the Crusaders and built up a flourishing trade in Eastern goods, which grew and prospered long after the last Crusaders had been driven out of Syria at the end of the thirteenth century. Their triumph in Jerusalem was short-lived. For barely ninety years they ruled the Holy City and kept a precarious hold on the small Crusader States along the Syrian coast. Then, with the rise of the great Kurdish warrior Saladin, the tide turned against them.

Saladin was brought up as a boy among the Seljuks of northern Syria and later served in Egypt as commander in chief of the army. In 1171 he deposed the last of the Fatimid caliphs and founded a new dynasty of his own in Egypt, owing allegiance to the Caliph of Baghdad. Then he dedicated himself to a Holy War against the Crusaders, and in 1187 he captured Jerusalem.

His followers tore down the Christian symbols from the Aqsa Mosque and the Dome of the Rock, and Saladin made the buildings more beautiful than ever by covering the inner walls with golden mosaics. He built a new *mihrab* in the mosque, and brought from Aleppo a cedarwood *mimbar,* or pulpit, which had been made ready for the reconquest of Jerusalem.

46

Saladin also renovated the gilding of the Dome of the Rock. Once more the building was swept and perfumed with rosewater twice a week—a service that kings were glad to perform—and on Fridays ten servants stood at the four entrances, calling to all people that the building was open for prayer. The people said their prayers as they paced around the Rock, between the arcades of gilded columns, under the brilliant new mosaics, and Moslem pilgrims came to worship there from as far away as Spain in the west and Persia in the east.

The land of Persia, many days' journey away by camel caravan across brown deserts and harsh bare mountains, was too distant to have felt the impact of the Crusades. The country was prospering under the rule of the Seljuk Turks, and with prosperity came a golden age of art and craftsmanship.

Opposite
METALWORK
OF EAST AND WEST:
Left BRONZE EWER
Mosan, 13th century
Right WINGED MONSTER
From a silver dish
Persian, 7th or 8th century

MIMBAR IN AL-AQSA MOSQUE
Made in Aleppo, Syria, 1168–74
(Photo: Creswell)

STAR TILE: PRINCE
AND ATTENDANTS
Kashan, 1211–12

the seljuk turks—
persia and mesopotamia

THE SELJUK TURKS were far more than fierce fighters and tireless horsemen. They carved out a mighty empire for themselves,
stretching over Persia, Mesopotamia, Asia Minor, and the
Caucasus. They founded a kingdom in Afghanistan, and by the
end of the eleventh century they had invaded India. The Seljuk
sultans were patrons of learning and friends of poets, scientists,
historians, and geographers. They established peace and security
within the borders of their realms, and wherever the Seljuks ruled,
they brought with them their bold and vigorous art.

The Great Seljuks of Persia chose as their capital the town of
Isfahan, an oasis in the high dry plateau of Central Persia. Like
Cairo, Isfahan owed its life to a river. The waters of the Zaindeh
Rud came down from the mountains to the west and spread
greenness over the plain of Isfahan. Gardens of fruit trees, nut
trees, and succulent melons surrounded the city, while a few miles
away there was only waterless desert. Caravan routes crossed the
desert to Isfahan from north and south, and the town must have
been a center of trade and crafts long before the Seljuk sultans
built their palace there.

48

SOUTHWEST IWAN OF THE FRIDAY MOSQUE, ISFAHAN

The Seljuk Palace and the great square, or Maidan, that lay before it have long since disappeared, but the ancient Friday Mosque, which also faced the square, still stands today. Unlike the mosques we have seen, it was not a rectangular building with a courtyard in front but was built on a new plan, which became typical of Persian mosques.

We enter the building today through a narrow dark passageway from the street. Suddenly we find ourselves in a vast central courtyard, lined with rows of pointed arches and dominated by four immense arched recesses, or *iwans*, opening off the four sides. The courtyard and *iwans* probably existed in Seljuk times, but the wonderful tiles that cover the walls and arches and make the courtyard into a paradise of color were added by Persian artists of later centuries. The mosque has been altered, repaired, and made more beautiful by generations of builders and decorators. To find the work of the Seljuk builders, just as they left it, we must turn in the direction of Mecca, pass under the *iwan* on the southwest side of the court, and enter the prayer hall within.

49

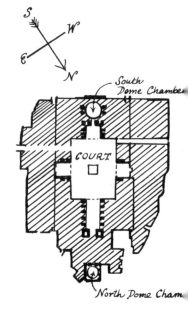

South Dome Chamber

COURT

North Dome Cham

THE FRIDAY MOSQUE: INTERIOR OF THE SMALL DOME CHAMBER

We stand under a colossal dome of grayish-brown bricks. All is simplicity, solidity, and strength. The structure itself provides the decoration, and looking up into the corners of the chamber, we can see how skillfully the builders bridged the corners with small arches and solved the difficult problem of placing a round dome on a square building. This great dome chamber was built in 1080 at the command of the famous vizier who served the Seljuk sultans Alp Arslan and Malik Shah. Renowned for wisdom and scholarship, he was always known by his title, Nizam-ul-Mulk, the Ordering of the Kingdom. There had been a mosque here long before his time, and probably the old buildings still stood around the new domed prayer hall.

A few years later, in 1088, a rival of Nizam-ul-Mulk added a second dome chamber at the opposite end of the mosque. It is smaller but even more beautiful in its simplicity and strength. Here again we see the patterns of small arches at the corners of the chamber. The decorations consist of Kufic inscriptions and bands of carved plaster, or stucco, set into the brickwork.

The two dome chambers, masterpieces of architecture, give us little idea of the Seljuks' delight in lavish ornament. They adorned

50

Opposite
PLAN OF THE
FRIDAY MOSQUE

PART OF A PANEL
OF STAR TILES
Persian,
13th century

their buildings with raised designs in brickwork and sculptured reliefs in stucco, and they covered the walls of rooms with glazed pottery tiles, painted in brilliant colors and gold luster. In Persia they needed color. So much of the land was desert, and flowers bloomed only during the brief spring, before the earth was scorched by the summer sun. The panels of painted tiles could fill the rooms of palaces and the *mihrabs* of mosques with springtime beauty, whatever the season.

The Persian potters in the towns of Kashan and Rayy were masters of the difficult art of making lusterware, and in the twelfth century they began to make magnificent luster tiles. These were often star-shaped; and cross-shaped pieces, of contrasting color, were made to fit between them. Tiles for the decoration of mosques were painted with arabesques and quotations from the Koran. In palaces, where pictures of figures were permitted, we would find star tiles like the one of the prince on page 48.

The pottery vessels made by the Seljuks were as beautiful as their tiles, and immensely varied in pattern and technique. Much of the pottery was made from a fine white paste in imitation of

POTTERY JUG
Kashan,
1215–16

the Chinese porcelain so popular in Persia. Bowls, jugs, cups, and vases were decorated with gold luster and colors, and often the designs were carved or molded in relief. A plain earthenware jug is clothed in an openwork shell of glazed pottery in black and turquoise and cobalt blue, with a vigorous design of deer and sphinxes, hares and hounds, all in a forest of intertwining leaves and stems. We even find ceramic sculpture in the round, brilliantly glazed in turquoise.

Some of the loveliest pottery of Rayy and Kashan was painted in enamels in as many as seven colors, a complicated process that involved several firings in the kiln. The number of colors and the delicate technique enabled the artists to paint designs of many small figures, often scenes of court life and hunting, which pleased the princely patrons for whom this pottery was made.

Above CERAMIC
FIGURE OF A MUSICIAN
Persian, 12th–13th century
Left LUSTER-PAINTED
BOWL *Rayy, 12th century*

EARTHENWARE BOWL:
BAHRAM GUR HUNTING
Kashan, 13th century

The subject of the painting on a splendid bowl is taken from
the *Shah Nama*, the great Book of Kings, written by the Persian
poet Firdausi in the tenth century and still to this day the most
famous of Persian poems. The *Shah Nama* tells the story of Iran
from the time of Adam to the Arab conquest, and is filled with
stories of heroes and their epic deeds. On this bowl we see the
hero Bahram Gur out hunting on his camel with his musician,
Azada, seated behind him, playing her harp. Azada challenged
him to shoot a gazelle in such a way that its hind leg was pinned
to its ear—a feat that he promptly performed. Azada was unim-
pressed by his skill, and in a rage he pushed her off the camel.
We see both incidents in the same picture. Azada rides the camel
and also lies prone on the ground below, while to the left is the
unfortunate gazelle.

The lively designs of birds and beasts, favored by the potters,
were also woven into silks and brocades, and in metalwork we
find similar patterns engraved, inlaid, or hammered in relief.
Golden pieces are rare; the craftsmen usually worked with bronze

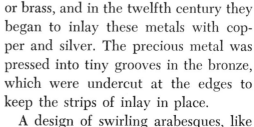

LION INCENSE BURNER
Persian, 1181–82

or brass, and in the twelfth century they began to inlay these metals with copper and silver. The precious metal was pressed into tiny grooves in the bronze, which were undercut at the edges to keep the strips of inlay in place.

A design of swirling arabesques, like interwoven ribbons, cover a magnificent brass ewer. Looking closely, we also find friezes of running animals and bands of Kufic script decorated with the heads of people at the tops of the upright strokes. Animal design on a large scale appears in a bronze incense burner in the shape of a lion, the body perforated in delicate openwork to let out the aromatic smoke of the incense. The sculptor of this lion, like the maker of the little deer from Medina az-Zahra, had no interest in representing a real animal. He smoothed out the contours and covered the whole body with a skin of intricate engravings that include an inscription, giving the name of the Seljuk prince who ordered the work, the name of the artist, and the date. It was made in 1181, probably in the province of northeastern Persia called Khorasan.

INLAID BRASS EWER
Persian, about 1200

54

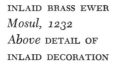

INLAID BRASS EWER
Mosul, 1232
Above DETAIL OF
INLAID DECORATION

From Persia this fine art of metalwork was carried westward to Mesopotamia and particularly to the city of Mosul. A fine brass ewer was made in 1232 for a ruler of Mosul, and is signed by its maker, a craftsman named Shuja of the same city. Inlaid with copper and silver, it is covered with geometric patterns, arabesques, animals, and lively human figures, such as the huntsman riding to the chase with his hound. A trained cheetah is perched behind him on the horse, ready to leap down and race after the gazelles of the desert.

Among the masterpieces of the Mosul metalworkers were oblong brass writing boxes for the use of scribes and wealthy scholars. The box shown on page 56 bears a Kufic inscription in praise of writing and scholarship, and in the row of medallions along the front are the signs of the zodiac. Inside the box are small covered cups for the ink and the sand, which served as blotting paper, and a long slot to hold reed pens.

55

INLAID BRASS WRITING BOX
Mosul, early 13th century

Many manuscripts must have been copied in Persia and Mesopotamia at the time this writing box was made, but few of them
have survived until today. The earliest Moslem miniatures known
appear in the *Andarz Nama,* a manuscript written and illustrated
at Gurgan in Persia between 1082 and 1090. Local Seljuk rulers,
called *atabegs,* probably employed professional scribes at their
courts to keep their libraries supplied with books, and at the
court of the caliph in Baghdad there was a flourishing school of
writing and illustration in the thirteenth century. Even scientific
treatises were given lively and colorful pictures. The doctor pre-
paring cough medicine comes from an Arabic translation of an
ancient Greek book, *Materia Medica,* on the medicinal uses of

DRAWING *From a
manuscript of the
Makamat
13th century*

RECIPE FOR COUGH MEDICINE *From a manuscript of the Materia Medica of Dioscorides 13th century*

herbs. There were also illustrated books of animal fables and splendid editions of the *Makamat,* a popular collection of tales about a quick-witted fellow called Abu Zaid, which gave the illustrators scope for their sense of humor.

The metalwork of Mosul was often made to order for rich men and princes in Aleppo, Damascus, and Cairo, and probably some of the manuscripts also were carried away along the old caravan roads to Syria and Egypt and north into Asia Minor. In the early thirteenth century the Seljuk kingdom in Asia Minor was enjoying a time of great prosperity under the wise rule of Sultan Alaeddin Keykubad. The sultan himself was not only a lover of books and scholarship but a good draftsman who could write an elegant script. He was also a carpenter and a maker of the short stiff bows that were used with such deadly aim by Turkish warriors.

Sultan Alaeddin's capital was the ancient town of Konya, called Iconium in Roman times. He had transformed it into a handsome city of mosques and religious schools, bazaars, inns, hospitals, and fine houses, interspersed with gardens and running streams. Scholars and poets and craftsmen of every kind were sure of a welcome there, and the citizens of the capital used to say with pride: "See all the world—but see Konya!"

STONE CARVING
OF A GRIFFIN
Seljuk, 13th century

the seljuk turks—asia minor

TRAVELERS TO Konya in the days of Sultan Alaeddin found a network of roads through the sultan's domains, winding over the mountains and across the windswept plateau of Anatolia, the heart of Asia Minor. The country was green with fields and gardens, and along the roads from town to town came merchant caravans of camels and mules, swinging along to the music of the camel bells and bringing merchandise from Persia, India, and China. Trade was the lifeblood of the sultan's kingdom, and the merchants had little to fear from robbers and bandits on the road. At night, even when darkness caught them far from a town, travelers could be sure of free lodging in one of the fortified inns, or *hans,* that stood by the roadside a convenient day's journey apart.

The largest *hans* were built by royal command. One of the most splendid, erected in the reign of Sultan Alaeddin, was the Sultan Han on the highway between Konya and the town of Aksaray to the north. Arriving weary after a long day on the road, travelers and their pack animals passed through the arched entrance of the *han* into a large inner courtyard. In the center of the court was a little mosque, set up on four stone piers and reached by a stone stairway, and on either side were rooms for travelers, each provided with a hearth for cooking. There were also a bath, a smithy, and storerooms for merchandise and fodder, while the

58

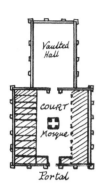

THE SULTAN HAN:
Above PLAN
Right GATEWAY

stables for the animals were at the far end of the court in a lofty hall with vaulted aisles. Servants were attached to the *han*, including musicians to entertain the guests in the evenings, and perhaps to wake them in the cold of early morning with a flourish of trumpets and drums.

Most *hans*, large and small, were built on this same general plan, though some of them had shops where merchants could lay out their wares and buy and sell as in a city bazaar. The architecture was plain and massive, and the decoration was usually concentrated on the gateways. The entrances of buildings were often given special importance by Turkish builders, and the gateway of the Sultan Han, which can still be seen today, is almost a counterpart of the noble *iwans* of Persian mosques.

There are zigzag moldings up the flanking pillars; the tall panels on either side are carved in relief patterns of lacelike delicacy, while the entrance arch itself is set back in a pointed recess with a "stalactite" design in the vault. This stalactite design was adopted by Moslem builders in many different countries, as we shall see. The Seljuk version is comparatively simple, made

59

MOSAIC TILE
Konya, 13th century

DESIGN OF STALACTITES

up of rows of little arches that give rather the effect of a cut-open honeycomb. Perhaps a clue to its origin may be found in the old Friday Mosque at Isfahan, if we remember the pattern of small arches in the corners of the two dome chambers.

The Turks in Asia Minor had broken loose from the rule of the Great Seljuks of Persia in the eleventh century, but in art and architecture their links with Persia were still strong. Persian artists came to Asia Minor, and among those who traveled to Konya to work for Sultan Alaeddin there were probably men of Kashan, skilled in the making of tiles.

Many fragments of luster tiles in the Persian style have been found in the ruins of Sultan Alaeddin's palace on the shore of a lake near Konya. Star-shaped tiles were painted with figures of people on horseback or sitting cross-legged, and with the lively animals we so often see in Seljuk art; and cross-shaped tiles of rich blue and black were made to fit between them. Luster tiles were too delicate and expensive for large-scale schemes of decoration, and when the tilemakers were called upon to decorate the mosques of Konya with glowing color, they worked in faïence mosaic.

Instead of the designs being painted on the tiles, they were built up with fragments of glazed tile of different colors, fitted together like a jigsaw puzzle. The pieces of the pattern were chipped off large tiles, each glazed in a single color, and were laid face downward on the design that was drawn on a sheet of paper. When the pattern was complete, mortar was poured over the back, binding the pieces together in a single panel.

Faïence mosaic could be made to fit over curved surfaces, even the complicated "stalactite" niches of *mihrabs*. The craftsmen at Konya used mostly tiles of turquoise and shades of blue and purple to make patterns of rosettes and stars, interlacing geometric arabesques and lines of ornate Kufic script. Later on, as we shall see, the same technique was used in more supple and flowing designs of many colors, which covered the walls of mosques and even spread over domes and minarets.

MOSAIC TILE
Konya, 13th century

Sultan Alaeddin's new buildings at Konya were also enriched with stone carvings in relief. We find carved peacocks, lions, and griffins, luxuriant curling plant forms, and strange creatures in which plant and animal are mixed. There are crude but vigorous carvings of warriors and seated figures, and sometimes impressive sculpture in the round.

STONE CARVING
Seljuk, 13th century

In wood the sculptors worked on a smaller scale and with great refinement, especially in making the furnishings for mosques. Intricately carved arabesques covered wooden doors, pulpits, and X-shaped reading stands that held the open Koran. The great Alaeddin Mosque at Konya was repaired and enlarged by Sultan Alaeddin, and when the work was finished in the year 1220, the sultan presented to the mosque a set of magnificent carpets for the floor. Some of them, preserved in the mosque for centuries, have survived until today.

61

CARVED WOODEN
KORAN STAND
Seljuk, 13th century

CARPET BORDER
Konya,
13th century

Fragments of carpets older than these have been found in Egypt and in Central Asia, and carpets were certainly made and used in the lands of the Arab Empire long before the thirteenth century. Persian rugs were famous in the Middle Ages, but none of the early ones have come down to us. The carpets from Konya are among the oldest surviving examples of the carpetmaker's craft.

CAMEL'S
HOOF

There is nothing primitive about them. They are large and brightly colored in red and pink, dark and light blue, pale green and yellow. Like the later carpets, the design of each one is divided into a central field surrounded by a border. In the centers are close-set geometric patterns of stars, squares, arabesques, and the eight-sided design known as the camel's hoof. The broad borders are often filled with Kufic script, so simplified and stylized that it becomes a bold and beautiful abstract design.

BORDER
DESIGN

The Konya carpets, like those of modern Turkey, were made by the technique called the Turkish knot. The carpet weavers

PART OF A
LARGE CARPET
WITH BORDER
OF STYLIZED
KUFIC SCRIPT
Konya,
13th century

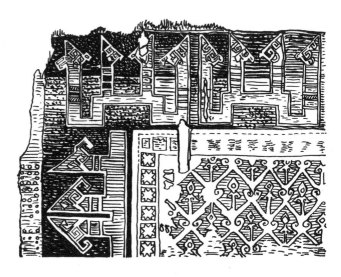

used an upright loom on which the strong warp threads were vertically stretched. The short lengths of colored wool, which formed the pattern, were each knotted around two threads of the warp and the ends pulled out to make a tuft. When the knotting was done and the whole warp covered, the woolen tufts were trimmed to an even length to give the carpet a smooth surface, sharpen the outlines of the design, and brighten the color.

The designers and makers of the Konya carpets were masters of their art with a long tradition behind them. The Turks had been making carpets in their homeland in Central Asia since early times, when their first efforts were crude imitations of furry animal skins. Carpetmaking was a favorite craft of nomad people. The materials were close at hand. They took the wool from their own flocks and the colors from the juices of plants. The finished carpets were easy to roll up and carry about from camp to camp, and when they were spread on the floor of a nomad's tent, they made it into a warm, comfortable, and colorful home. As the Turks moved westward, they carried with them their skill in carpet weaving, and when they were converted to Islam, their splendid rugs found a new use in the mosques, covering the floors where the faithful knelt to pray.

TURKISH KNOT

The carpets presented to the mosque at Konya are treasures of Seljuk art, a gift worthy of the great Sultan Alaeddin. After his death in 1237, architecture and the arts continued to flourish in Asia Minor, but already the threat of a new and terrible invasion had arisen in the East. Another Asian people, the Mongols, had burst from the distant country of the steppes to invade the rich lands of the Arab Empire. Their leader, Chingiz Khan, had sworn to be lord of the world, and no army could stand against the fury of his attack.

By 1227, when their leader died, the Mongols had ravaged Central Asia, destroyed the cities of Bukhara and Samarkand, and overrun the province of Khorasan, crushing the last remnants of Seljuk power in Persia. Soon they were gathering their forces to drive through to Europe. They invaded the Caucasus and southern Russia, and in 1243 they tore into Asia Minor and forced the

63

BACKGROUND
PATTERNS OF
KONYA CARPETS

Seljuks there to become their vassals. In 1258 came the worst blow of all—the destruction of Baghdad and the slaughter of the caliph.

The Moslem world was stunned with horror. Moslems and Christians alike trembled in terror of the inhuman invaders, like centaurs on their tireless horses, burning, looting, and slaying defenseless citizens by the thousands. The destruction left by the Mongols was terrible, the slaughter beyond belief. Cities were not only sacked but leveled to the ground. Priceless works of art were gone forever. Ruins were littered with shards of broken pottery. Libraries were burned or the books torn up to serve as bedding for the conquerors' horses.

At last, when they invaded Palestine in 1260, the Mongols were confronted by the army of Qutuz, Sultan of Egypt. Commanded by the brilliant Turkish general Baybars, the Egyptian army met the Mongols at the Battle of Goliath's Spring and hurled them back. The Mongols retreated to the ravished lands of Iraq and Persia, driven out of Syria by Baybars' furious attack. The Egyptians marched home victorious, and on the way Baybars murdered the sultan and seized the throne of Egypt for himself. Baybars had been a slave at the Egyptian court; now he was the fourth and greatest of the Mamluk sultans, the "slave dynasty" that was to rule Egypt until the sixteenth century.

He had saved Egypt from the Mongols, with its treasures of art and architecture untouched. Cairo, his capital, was a refuge for the artists and craftsmen of the Near East who had fled before the Mongol invasion. Their skill contributed to a wonderful flowering of art in Egypt, while in the blackened ruins of Baghdad and the wasted cities of Persia it seemed as though art could never rise again.

TURKISH
WARRIOR
*From a
Turkish
manuscript,
15th century*

egypt and syria under the mamluks

SULTAN BAYBARS of Egypt was a patron of the arts as well as a
warrior. He lived in unparalleled magnificence, and to see him
ride forth in state through the streets of Cairo no one would
believe that he had begun life as a slave.

Clad in black silk with a snow-white turban, the sultan rode
in the midst of a glittering procession. He was preceded by a lord
carrying the royal saddlecloth, sewn with gold and jewels, and
by two pages on white horses, dressed in yellow silk with borders
of gold brocade. Beside him rode a mace-bearer with a gold-
headed mace, and over the sultan's head a prince held a ceremonial umbrella of yellow silk, embroidered with gold and
crowned by a golden bird. The troops who protected the sultan
were also in silk, blazoned with the arms of their leaders, and
ministers of state rode in robes of brocade. A flute player marched
ahead, and a singer chanted the stories of bygone heroes to the
rhythm of a hand drum; or, for great occasions, there would be
the stirring music of the sultan's band—four large drums and
forty kettledrums, four oboes and twenty trumpets.

Cairo, Baybars' capital, was a far greater city than in the
days of the Fatimid caliphs, and refugees, fleeing before the
Mongols, had swelled the population. Saladin, during his rule
in Egypt in the twelfth century, had conceived the idea of building a mighty wall to unite the Fatimid palace-city with old
Fustat, a mile to the south. His wall began at the river port of
El-Maqs on the Nile, ran eastward to link up with the walls of
the Fatimid city, and then turned south, following the line of the

BRASS BOWL
INLAID WITH SILVER
Egyptian
Late 13th century

Muqattam Hills. The eastern side of the wall was backed by cliffs, and on a lofty spur Saladin built a fortress, the Citadel. His city wall ended just north of the fortress and was never completed; the Citadel, finished after Saladin's death, became an impregnable stronghold, in the style of the greatest Crusader castles in Syria. It was built by the toil of Frankish prisoners captured in the Crusades, using stone from the ancient pyramids of Giza, and for centuries the rulers of Cairo had their palaces within its walls.

The fortress commanded a view of the whole city. Below the sheer face of the fortress rock lay an open square surrounded by mosques and the houses of the rich. In the time of the Mamluks part of the square was a busy market for horses and donkeys; next to this were the sultans' stables, and at the southern end their polo ground, reached by a private stairway from the Citadel. Sultan Baybars was an expert at the Persian game of polo. As energetic in his pleasures as he was in war, he delighted in hawking and archery, horse racing and tournaments with the lance, and he held tremendous feasts at his palace in the Citadel. Roast sheep, pigeons and fowls were piled on the dishes to the height of a man, and, as in Fatimid times, the tables were adorned with fantastic sculpture in sugar. Singers and dancers entertained the guests, and wine was served in plenty.

A special cup for drinking parties is pictured in an Egyptian manuscript devoted to mechanical inventions. The metal bird perched on the cover is supposed to turn and whistle when the cup is filled with wine—the kind of device that had delighted Moslem rulers since the days of Harun ar Rashid.

Some of the stories of the *Arabian Nights* were probably written in Egypt in the fourteenth century, and they reflect the wealth and splendor of the Mamluk court. The rooms of the sultan's palace were furnished with rich carpets, silken cushions and draperies, tables of metal and carved wood and thrones of ivory; lamps and chests of shining silver; and vessels of brass adorned with inscriptions and lively scenes in silver inlay. Craftsmen who had fled from Mosul before the invasion of the Mongols carried on their fine inlay work in Egypt and Syria, and in Cairo there was a special Market of the Inlayers during the thirteenth and fourteenth centuries. Ewers, trays, and incense burners of inlaid metal offered scope for the most intricate designs. A brass bowl for hand-washing is decorated with tiny figures of men drinking and playing music, riding elephant and camel and duck hunting by boat. Even a round brass handwarmer was transformed into a thing of beauty, inlaid with arabesques, bold inscriptions, and two-headed eagles, the owner's coat of arms.

INLAID BRASS HANDWARMER
Syrian, 1264–79

DESIGN FOR A CUP *From a 14th-century Egyptian manuscript*

The makers of glassware, whose masterpieces had so impressed the Crusaders in Syria, mostly worked in Aleppo and Damascus. They painted their clear glass vessels with gold and brilliant enamels—red, yellow, green, blue and pink. The designs were often arranged in bands, showing drinkers and musicians and running animals. This lovely bottle, gilded and enameled, has an unusual frieze of warriors in battle. Perhaps they represent the Egyptians fighting the Mongols, for some wear turbans and others, Mongol caps and helmets.

The glassmakers of Syria and Egypt also made exquisite lamps for mosques. These were shaped like vases, swelling out in a globe at the bottom and flared at the top. The wick burned in a cup of olive oil that rested in a bowl of water in the bottom of the lamp, and there were small glass loops on the outside for the chains by which the lamp was hung from the ceiling or from a bracket on the wall. Every mosque had many lamps, and the soft glow of light through the painted glass must have been magically beautiful. The lamps were patterned with flowers and inscriptions from the Koran and often bore the coats of arms of the rich men who had paid for their making.

Above GLASS BOTTLE
Egyptian, 14th century
Below GLASS MOSQUE LAMP
Syrian, 13th century

DESIGN FROM A BOOK COVER
Egyptian, 14th century

PAGE FROM THE KORAN
Egyptian, 14th century

The mosques were also adorned with wooden *mimbars,* even more elaborately ornamented than the one presented by Saladin to the Aqsa Mosque in Jerusalem. They were covered with star-shaped panels fitted together, no two alike, filled with minute arabesques, and often inlaid with slender strips of bone or ivory or with different kinds of wood.

The same geometric patterns were worked on leather book-bindings and enriched with gold tooling by the craftsmen of Egypt and North Africa, who had long been famous for leather-work. Sometimes the designs of the covers were cut out in leather and placed on a colored background, while the flaps that folded over the front edges of the books were stamped with intricate arabesques. The manuscripts protected by these fine covers were no longer copied in the majestic Kufic writing but in the more rounded and flowing form of Arabic script known as Nakshi, which was combined with curling arabesque illumination in gold and colors.

Many magnificent Korans must have been copied for the Mamluk sultans. Pleasure-loving though they were, the Mamluks

GREAT GATE
OF THE MADRASA
OF SULTAN HASAN,
CAIRO

and their followers were devoutly religious men and builders of mosques, domed tombs, hospitals, and schools. Since the days of the Fatimids, Cairo had been a center of religious teaching, and students from all over the Moslem world flocked to study there. The religious schools, called *madrasas,* were built on a special plan, introduced into Egypt by Saladin. The buildings of the *madrasa* were arranged around a courtyard with four great *iwans,* and with a domed prayer hall on the side facing Mecca. Saladin had seen buildings like this by Seljuk architects in Syria, but we can trace the design eastward to Persia, for it takes us back to the plan of the Friday Mosque at Isfahan.

The huge *madrasa* built in the reign of Sultan Hasan in the fourteenth century is one of the most awe-inspiring buildings in Cairo. It stands near the square before the Citadel, and the entrance portal rises to a dizzying height above the narrow street below. The outer walls of the *madrasa* are adorned with tall

70

narrow windows and an immense jutting cornice at the top. Only the portal is richly decorated, and it recalls, on an enormous scale, the gateway of the Sultan Han. As we gaze up into the recess of the arch, we see there the familiar stalactite pattern, another gift from Seljuk art.

Up the steps and through the mighty arch, we come into a domed hall, pass along a vaulted passageway around several sharp corners, and emerge at last into the central courtyard with the four colossal *iwans*. The great court is almost bare of decoration, except for the stone battlements along the tops of the walls and the inscriptions around the archway that leads into the sanctuary. The walls of the court, so high they shut out the sun, are covered with stucco, stern and plain, as though the scholars who studied there must have no distractions from their books and meditations. The labyrinth of rooms where the students and their teachers lived and worked are hidden behind the corners of the court. They form four distinct sections fitted into the angles of the cross made by the court and *iwans*, and each section was used by a different school of Moslem religious teaching.

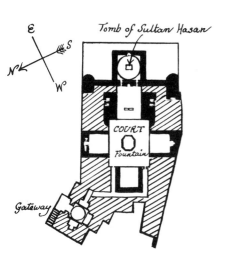

THE MADRASA OF
SULTAN HASAN:
Above PLAN
Right COURTYARD

When we compare the restrained grandeur of this mighty building with the miniature delicacy of the glassware, metalwork, and wood carving of Mamluk times, we begin to see the richness and variety of Egyptian art in the thirteenth and fourteenth centuries. As Egypt was the gathering place for artists from all over the Near East, those who worked in Cairo could draw upon a great pool of ideas in Moslem art and architecture; but if we look closely at their work, we discover traces of a strange foreign influence from far beyond the Moslem world.

CHINESE
LOTUS
PATTERN

We find free and rhythmic flower designs woven into a fourteenth century silk, painted on a mosque lamp and inlaid on a metal bowl. Around the neck of a glass bottle is a flying phoenix, a mythical bird from China. The peonies, lotus flowers, and chrysanthemums found in the patterns of textiles, glass, and metalwork in the Near East are Chinese flowers. The Mamluks, with their passion for silk, imported silken textiles and brocades that appear to have been made in China or in Central Asia and that combine in their decoration Chinese dragons and parrots with Arabic inscriptions.

These are small clues, but they tell an exciting story of intercourse between East and West across the vast lands of the Mongol Empire. Egypt was never conquered by the Mongols, but it could not escape the far-ranging influence of their art. When we turn to the Mongol Kingdom of Persia, we shall see how even these people, the greatest destroyers the world had ever known, brought new inspiration, new life and beauty to Moslem art.

14TH-CENTURY
EGYPTIAN
FLORAL DESIGNS
*From a mosque
lamp (right)
From a brass
bowl (left)*

وأظهر أبو القسم بن سيجور وجهله فيلذلقم ودبقة الأسال دائن دين بي بصر وكذلك اسرنورناث الحاجب الذي كان ساعد المنصر ومعينه
وركنه الادى واجهزاكة العسكر وجهز العسكر اللذين في لبان العاردتا كنا وانهزم المنصر كنايرا لغارية اخطارا لمهالك واقطاعا
الماك وجه الامير نصره كف الاشال والدولهوعيا السايدوالنصرة لا مسترعة الي الاعوزة فتاهؤامقنه
بسبب قله كانت بنهم وبيه ودحلوا في طاعة ومشوا خذمة لوابه الى بلاد الكهان واسرؤاجماعة من عشكره وقتلوالحظنا منهم بالسيف

the mongols and the road to china

THE MIGHTY EMPIRE of the Mongols, stretching from Persia to
China, was divided among the descendants of Chingiz Khan,
princes who owed allegiance to Kublai Khan in China but were
virtually independent rulers. The Il-Khan Baraga, lord of Persia,
chose Baghdad as his capital, and new buildings began to rise
from the ruins of the round city of the caliphs. The conquered
lands were slowly recovering from the terror of the invasion.
Farmers returned to their fields and craftsmen to their shops. The
town of Rayy and some of the other battered cities of northern
Persia would never regain their former state, but Isfahan and
Shiraz in the south had escaped destruction, and even in the
ravaged north the conquerors had often spared the lives of craftsmen.

The Mongols were nomads with few crafts of their own. They

73 MONGOL WARRIORS *From a manuscript of
Rashid ad Din's History of the World, 1307*

depended on the skill of the people they conquered, and they had a deep respect for craftsmen, particularly metalworkers who could make armor and weapons. Persia was already a country of fine craftsmen and artists, and the Mongols brought in skilled workers from China along the old Silk Road, the path of caravans across Asia from the Far East.

In the days of the Roman Empire, this had been the route along which the treasured silks of China came to Western Europe, but for centuries after the fall of the empire, the Silk Road had been dangerous and often impassable, beset by bandits and warring tribesmen. Now, in the thirteenth century, the whole way lay within the Mongols' vast domains. The caravan routes were almost cleared of robbers; merchants with their precious loads of silks and spices could pass in safety; and even adventurers from Europe could take the road to China.

In 1272 Marco Polo and his father and uncle set out on their famous journey across the deserts, steppes, and mountains of Asia to the court of Kublai Khan in Peking. Marco Polo saw with his own eyes how the Mongols were bringing peace and order to the wild lands in the heart of Asia; how they had linked up distant corners of their empire by a system of swift messengers, and had established a standard currency to encourage trade. The Polos carried golden tablets of safe-conduct from Kublai Khan, which served as passports and ensured them the best service at inns and posthouses where fresh horses could be found for the journey. The Mongols welcomed men from the West, whether they were missionaries, merchants, or craftsmen. The way was open for travelers from the Mediterranean to the Yellow Sea, and like the roads of the old Arab Empire, the caravan routes across Asia were paths for ideas, new ideas in art flowing westward from China to the lands of the Near East and the Mediterranean shore.

The Persian city of Tabriz was the meeting place for merchants from East and West. Men of Baghdad came there to buy precious stones from merchants of India or to sell pearls and silks to enterprising Venetians and Genoese. Marco Polo, passing through

Tabriz, called it a "large and noble city . . . surrounded with delightful gardens which produce the finest fruits," and the Mongol rulers of Persia had chosen it as their summer residence. They kept their old nomadic habit of moving with the seasons, and the cool mountain air of Tabriz was a welcome change from the heat of Baghdad.

Ghazan Khan, who came to the throne in 1295, made Tabriz into a center of Moslem scholarship and art as well as commerce. Before his reign few Mongols had been converted to Islam. Some were Buddhists, and others had listened to the preaching of Christian missionaries from Europe; but Ghazan Khan formally declared himself to be a Moslem, and decreed that the many ruined mosques in towns and villages throughout Persia should be rebuilt.

The Mongols turned to building with the same fiery energy that had made them such terrible destroyers. They rebuilt entire towns, flattened by the invasion, making wide, spacious streets, strong walls for defense, and ample markets and caravansaries for merchants. On the south side of Tabriz, Ghazan Khan built a new suburb which included religious schools and a library, a hospital, a palace, and wide-spreading gardens. Meanwhile Rashid ad Din, the khan's great prime minister, had laid out his own suburb east of the city. Here, among the hundreds of houses and shops, were special accommodations for scholars. Students, calligraphers, and illuminators of books were welcomed there and given free lodging and money for their living expenses. Artists from Mesopotamia and Persia began to flock to Tabriz and to the neighboring cities of Maragha and Sultaniya.

Rashid ad Din, a scholar himself, wrote a history of the Mongols and a history of the world. He had a number of copies made, and parts of the World History survive today with the original pictures. In the illustration shown on page 73 we see the famous Mongol cavalry drawn up for battle in a landscape represented by a single fantastic rock. On their small sturdy horses, the warriors wait, tense and expectant, ready to charge. Using few colors, chiefly brown and gray and silver with touches of red and blue, the artist shows us every detail of their armor, helmets, and weapons, and makes an exciting pattern of the long lances and banners that break out of the picture into the margins of the page.

Among the oldest Persian miniatures are the illustrations for the *Description of Animals*, which was copied at Maragha in 1299, by order of Ghazan Khan. The book deals with the habits of animals and the medical uses of animal products. True natural history is mixed with ancient legends, and we learn such surprising things as that deer are fond of music but detest snakes and will fight them to the death.

Some of the illustrations are in the flat, brightly colored style of the old Baghdad school, but most of them are painted in a new free technique with muted color, and in these we see the influence of China. The Chinese artists of the thirteenth century often painted in ink, using only subtle grays and blacks, and they were close observers of nature and master painters of landscape, flowers, and animals. We know that the Mongols brought many paintings and woodcuts from China, and the Persian book artists

GIRAFFE *From a manuscript of the Description of Animals Maragha, 1299*

FUNERAL OF ISFANDYAR *From a manuscript of the Shah Nama*
Persian, about 1320

must have studied them and learned to take a fresh view of
nature. In the *Description* we find pictures of animals so full of
rhythm and movement they might have been painted from life.
The giraffe is particularly well drawn, and when we remember
that the rulers of those days often kept menageries of exotic beasts,
it is tempting to think that the artist actually saw a giraffe at
Baghdad or Tabriz.

The Chinese influence can be traced again in the illustrations
for a splendid manuscript of the *Shah Nama*, the Book of Kings,
made in Tabriz in 1320. This picture is a scene of mourning for a
dead hero. His body is carried on a litter surrounded by mourners
in a passion of grief, their hair flowing loose and their faces
tense with emotion. The flying birds and the scroll pattern of

77

POLO GAME *From a manuscript of the Shah Nama, Shiraz, 1341*

clouds are common Chinese motifs, but it is the clean, vibrant lines of the drawing that show us the blending of Chinese and Persian art into a new style.

In contrast to this great and powerful picture are the illustrations for a much smaller *Shah Nama*, made in 1341 in Shiraz, capital of the southern province of Fars. Here the colors are mainly red and yellow, and the drawing is light and sketchy. The riders are playing a game of polo, favorite sport of the Persians, and their horses gallop against a flat red background.

Shiraz, already famous as a city of gardens, poets, and nightingales, was ruled at this time by the turbulent Inju family, who had broken loose from the domination of the Il-Khan in Tabriz. Their city had grown wealthy through the revival of the old sea-borne trade with China, for it lay on the route of northbound caravans coming across the desert from Ormuz on the Persian Gulf, the port for the China trade.

Persian potters, like the miniature painters, borrowed ideas from Chinese art. In the early years of Mongol rule, the potters went on working in the styles of Seljuk times. Then they began to use free swirling designs, as in this bowl with leaping hares and tall grasses. We find pottery decorated with peonies and lotus blossoms, scroll-shaped cloud bands, and flying birds. Figures of hares, deer, and people in Mongol dress were placed against a background of small curled leaves, and sometimes the designs were raised in low relief. The potters used the same muted colors as the miniature painters of Tabriz and Baghdad— black and gray, turquoise, purple, and blue; and for wall decoration they made beautiful luster tiles, often modeled in relief.

DRUG JAR
Persian
14th century

78

EARTHENWARE DISH
Persian, early 14th century
Right BOWL WITH DESIGN
OF LEAPING HARES
Persian, late 13th century

TILE WITH BIRDS
AND SCRIPT
PAINTED IN
LUSTER AND BLUE
Kashan, 1309

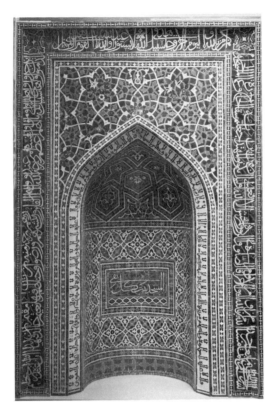

MIHRAB OF FAÏENCE
MOSAIC *From the
Madrasa Imami,
Isfahan, 1354*

Many *mihrabs* in mosques were adorned with luster tiles or with faïence mosaic in patterns of flowers, geometric arabesques, and bands of script. The Mongols also decorated their buildings with fine carving in stone and stucco. One of their masterpieces is the exquisite *mihrab* of carved stucco that was placed in the Friday Mosque at Isfahan in the time of the Il-Khan Uljaitu.

Uljaitu's domed tomb at Sultaniya is a huge brick building, decorated inside with faïence mosaic and painted stucco. Besides erecting his own tomb, Uljaitu repaired and partly rebuilt the Shrine of the Imam Reza in the northeastern province of Khorasan. The buildings of the shrine surrounded the tomb of the young holy man, the eighth of the Twelve Imams revered by Persian Moslems, who died—or was murdered—there in the year 818. Soon after his death his tomb became a center of pilgrimage, and the small town that grew up around the shrine was called Meshed, meaning "place of martyrdom."

80

TOMB OF AL-GAZZALI
AT TUS, NEAR MESHED

The Mongol khans and their followers built a number of handsome domed tombs, and one of these, small but strangely impressive, still stands today a few miles northwest of Meshed. It was built about 1320, in memory of a Persian saint and religious thinker, al-Gazzali. Rising abruptly from the flat plain of fields, the building is the same sandy-brown color as the surrounding land. Almost the only decorations outside are tall recessed panels in the brick walls and ropelike moldings at the corners. Windows of brick openwork let in the sunlight in spots and splashes, and within there are stucco reliefs of leaves and lotus blossoms. At the four corners of the building spiral stairways lead up to the tops of the walls around the base of the dome. From there we look out over the plain, ringed by the bare mountains of Khorasan, while away to the east is the way to Samarkand, the Silk Road to China, and the path of the Mongol invasions.

This lonely building and a mound of crumbling mud walls and towers are all that is left of the town of Tus, birthplace of the poet Firdausi who wrote the *Shah Nama*. At the end of the fourteenth century, when the Mongol Kingdom in Persia was broken up among warring princes, a new invading army came sweeping in along the old path of conquest. It was the army of Timur the Lame, known to the West as Tamerlane, and today the ruins of Tus, littered with broken fragments of Mongol pottery, tell us of the terror of his passing.

From their homeland in Central Asia, Timur's raiding armies looted, slaughtered, and plundered east and west, cutting again the road between Europe and China. They stabbed deep into India and sacked the city of Delhi in 1398. They raged across Persia, and by 1402 Timur was in Syria and had raided Damascus. He scored a victory over the Mamluks of Egypt and routed the Ottoman Turks, successors of the Seljuks, in Asia Minor. Again it seemed as though the civilization of the East would be wiped out and its art destroyed in the smoke of burning cities.

Distant Spain, of all the countries of the old Arab Empire, was safely beyond the reach of Timur's onslaught, but there the Moslems held only a remnant of their once-great kingdom of al-Andalus. The Caliphate of Córdoba had long ago been abolished, and for centuries the Christians had been pressing down from the north, gradually winning back the land they had lost to the Arabs. In vain the Moslem princes called in Berbers from Morocco to help them in the fight. The newcomers carved out kingdoms for themselves in Spain, but still the Christian conquest went on. In 1236 Córdoba fell to Ferdinand III of Castile, and Seville was vanquished twelve years later. By the fourteenth century only the city of Granada and its small kingdom were left. Granada was doomed to fall to the Christians at the end of the fifteenth century, but in its last years under Moslem rule the city was adorned with exquisite art, and the Nasrid sultans of Granada revived in their embattled kingdom the past splendor of al-Andalus.

PHOENIX
From a
Persian
luster tile
14th century

GRanaӠa, last mooRish kingdom in spain

GRANADA IS A mountain city, well suited to be a stronghold.
Behind it rise the snow-capped peaks and ridges of the Sierra
Nevada, and in front lies the broad fertile plain of the Vega, so
green and lush that Arab chroniclers called Granada a "goblet
full of emeralds." They were never tired of praising the city, its
beauty beyond compare, its rivers like necklaces of pearls, its
wonderful fruits and blossoming gardens; but the greatest glory
of Granada was the Alhambra, the Red Palace of the Nasrid
sultans, which crowned the rocky hill above the river Darro.

The hill of the Alhambra had been a fortified place since early
times. When the first of the Nasrids, Muhammad Ibn al-Ahmar,
seized control of Granada in 1238, he strengthened the hilltop
fort and in the shelter of its walls he built his palace, looking
out over the town across the river. Successive Nasrid sultans
altered and added to Muhammad's palace, while the town of
Granada grew and prospered under their rule. From their high
windows the sultans could look down with pride on their capital;
its strong encircling walls with their many towers; the twisting

VIEW OF
GRANADA
AND THE
ALHAMBRA

network of streets, so narrow that two horsemen could hardly pass abreast; the minarets of mosques and the little clustered domes of public baths; and the great silk market where merchants from far and near came to buy the famous Grenadine silks and jewelry and gold brocade.

The whitewashed houses in the bright sunshine gave Granada the look of a North African town, such as the flourishing city of Fez in Morocco, but unlike the rulers of Fez, the Nasrids were not famous for their religious fervor or for the building of mosques and *madrasas*. They preferred the pleasures of the present life to the anticipation of the joys of Paradise, and their architectural masterpiece was their dreamlike palace, the Alhambra.

It was Muhammad V, in the fourteenth century, who made the Alhambra the lovely building it is today. Under the hands of his builders and decorators, many of them Christian craftsmen, the private apartments of the palace became a paradise of fantastic beauty, while the public rooms were designed to impress and humble all who entered. The Alhambra was a seat of government as well as a private refuge for the sultan and his household. The walls and towers surrounding the hilltop enclosed a complete fortified town with the Alcazaba, the ancient fortress, jutting out on the western spur of the hill. Ambassadors and their retinues, both Christian Spaniards and Moslems from North Africa, rode up the steep hill to the palace to discuss affairs of state, and the people of the sultan's kingdom came to ask for justice and the righting of wrongs.

They passed through the great walls by the Gate of Justice and rode on, still higher, to the horseshoe arch of the Wine Gate before the Alcazaba. The entrance to the palace itself faced west toward the towers of the fortress. Those who gained admittance were conducted across a courtyard with a small mosque in the southwest corner, through a second court and into the Hall of Mexuar, the meeting place of the Royal Council.

This small pillared hall is the first building we see when we enter the Alhambra today. For many years after the Christian conquest of Granada it was used as a chapel, and the brightly colored tiles and carved stucco that covered the walls have been damaged and much restored. In this hall the sultan's subjects presented their grievances; the ambassadors passed on to the second, and far more splendid, part of the palace, which centers upon the Court of Myrtles and the sultan's audience chamber.

A long pool, banked on either side by dark green hedges, stretches from end to end of the Court of Myrtles. The porch of round arches in front of the Hall of Ambassadors and the battle-mented tower that rises above are reflected in the water. The throne room and the reflecting pool may remind us of Abd er-Rahman's audience hall at Medina az-Zahra, but there the pool and the porch of horseshoe arches were on a large, impressive scale, and the walls of the throne room were faced with carved stonework and panels of marble. Here, the architecture is small and refined, and the decoration of the walls is of frail carved stucco and glazed tiles.

THE ALHAMBRA: COURT OF MYRTLES, LOOKING TOWARD THE AUDIENCE CHAMBER

THE ALHAMBRA:
AUDIENCE CHAMBER

On the wall above the slender columns of the porch, the stucco is worked into a pattern of diamond shapes, fine as lace. Crossing the porch, we enter a narrow anteroom where court officials and guards used to await the sultan's pleasure, and before us is the Hall of Ambassadors.

When the sultan gave audience here, a silken curtain would hang over the round archway leading into the hall. As this was drawn aside, the envoys would see the sultan enthroned in front of the deeply recessed window opposite the entrance. The windows were filled with richly colored glass that let in only a dim and filtered light. Glass lamps hung on chains from the carved and painted ceiling; the floor was spread with carpets, and the walls glowed with the brilliance of tiles and the gold, red, and green of painted stucco reliefs.

Today, as we stand in the Hall of Ambassadors, the glassless windows open on a view of the old town far below. We hear the sound of barking dogs and street cries and children playing, and the white light floods across the bare floor and reveals in hard outline the amazing decoration of the walls. From the dado of tiles to the lofty ceiling, every inch of the walls is covered with

interlacing arabesques, some in leafy vegetable forms, others like woven straps or ribbons; tiny lacy designs and large geometric star shapes; medallions and bands filled with Arabic inscriptions and the motto of Muhammad V: "There is no conqueror but Allah." Even with the color gone and the stucco bone-white, the impression is overwhelming.

In the third part of the palace, the rooms of the sultan and his household, we reach the climax of refinement and decoration. The rooms are grouped around the Court of Lions, the sultan's private paradise, shut away from the trials of the world. The small courtyard, with its central fountain in a stone basin supported by twelve lions, is divided into quarters by four little water channels representing the four rivers of Paradise. Everywhere there is the music of little fountains. Water flows into the court down flights of shallow steps from fountains in adjoining rooms, and water pours from the mouths of the lions into the narrow channels. Every flat piece of wall, however small, is worked into filigree patterns of infinite variety and complexity.

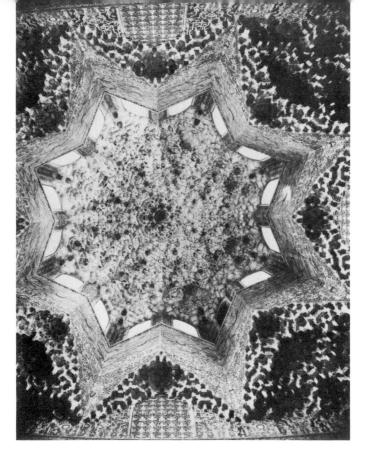

Even the arcades around the court are varied in design, with single columns and groups of twos and threes, round arches and pointed arches with their edges cut away in stalactites.

Here we see the final development of the stalactite pattern that we have followed from its simple beginnings in Persia to Asia Minor and to Egypt. The pattern, as we have seen, began as part of the structure and was carried out in brick or stone, which imposed simplicity and strength. When the Moroccan builders in Fez adopted the design in the twelfth century, they lined the dome of a mosque with stalactites made of plaster, forming a shell that concealed the structure underneath. The architects of the Alhambra took up the same idea of separating ornament from structure, but they went far beyond the Moroccan builders in complications of design. If we stand in the little chamber south of the Court of Lions, and look up at the amazing star-shaped

EL PARTAL,
FROM THE SOUTH

cupola above, we find the form so broken up into hundreds of tiny cells and pendants that it seems as though the solidity of real architecture has been dissolved away.

More stalactite vaults roof the long narrow Hall of Kings, east of the court, and the arches that punctuate the hall are all edged with stalactites. Opening off this hall are little alcoves, perhaps used as bedchambers, and on their smooth vaults, shaped like upturned boats, are paintings dim with age. They were probably painted by a Spanish or Italian artist of the fourteenth century, and show us the Nasrid sultans enthroned in their robes and turbans, a skirmish between Christians and Moors, and a boar hunt in which they join in friendly rivalry.

The rooms of the harem were north of the Court of Lions, and also in a small separate building, El Partal, sometimes called the Tower of the Ladies. This is made up of a little portico with several rooms within, facing a garden and a broad reflecting pool. From the windows on the north side of El Partal the ladies could gaze over the town to the distant mountains. To the east they looked across the deep ravine of the Darro to the neighboring hill of the Generalife, the Lofty Garden, one of the many small palaces that crowned the hills around Granada.

89

NASRID SULTAN
*From a 14th century
painting in the
Hall of Kings*

THE GENERALIFE:
COURT OF THE POOL

In the hot summers the sultan and some of his family and courtiers would cross from the Alhambra to the cool heights of the Generalife by a bridge over the Darro ravine. The bridge has long since disappeared, but the white buildings and two courtyards of the Generalife look very much as they did in the fourteenth century. The long narrow Court of the Pool, with a canal and small fountains down the center, recalls the Court of Myrtles, and the small pavilions at each end are decorated in the style of the Alhambra.

For coolness in the summer heat, the palace was enlivened by the ripple and sparkle of running streams, indoors and out. The stairway down the hillside through the terraced gardens had a fountain on each landing and water channels hollowed out in the tops of the parapets so that cascades rushed down on either side. There was even a lawn where hidden pipes sprayed jets of water over passers-by, a device that was later copied by European gardeners of the Renaissance.

The beauty of the Moorish palaces, in which house and garden were one, made a deep impression on Christian builders in Spain. Christian kings in the conquered cities often employed Moslem craftsmen to build houses in the Moorish style, such as the palace of King Pedro the Cruel in the Alcazar at Seville. The custom of having enclosed patio gardens became typical of Christian Spain, and was eventually brought by the Spaniards to America.

The Christians in Spain and Portugal also adopted from the Moors the use of glazed tiles as decoration in houses and gardens. Blue, the favorite color for Moorish tiles, was combined with gold luster by the potters of Granada who made the splendid tiles for the Alhambra and for the houses of wealthy citizens.

The art of making luster pottery was passed on to Spain from Egypt, and in the fourteenth century the Spanish port of Malaga, famous for its raisins, wines and honey-sweet figs, became equally well known for lusterware. Some of the Malaga potters moved to Manises on the east coast of Spain, and here, all through the fifteenth century, they produced handsome lusterware dishes and bowls and the tall drug jars of Persian design, called *albarellos,* which were used in apothecaries' shops to store rare drugs from the East.

Such lovely bowls as this one, with a vivid painting of a Portuguese warship, were intended for display in the dining halls of the rich. The pottery was often made to order and we find many fine pieces painted with the coats of arms of noble Italian families. These wonderful wares from Spain inspired the potters of Italy in the fifteenth

LUSTERWARE
DRUG-JAR
(ALBARELLO)
*Manises, early
15th century*

LUSTERWARE
BOWL *Manises,
early 15th century*

century. They learned the Spanish technique of tin glazing and painting and began to produce the brightly colored earthenware known as majolica.

Moorish silks were as famous as Moorish pottery. Most of the wealth of Granada came from its manufacture of silks and brocades, which were known and treasured as far away as England. Many of these fabrics were designed in the "Alhambra style," with interlacing bands, geometric patterns and inscriptions, like the tile and stucco decorations of the palace; but in the fourteenth century Chinese lotus designs also appeared in Spanish brocades.

The influence of Chinese art, brought in by the Mongols, had finally reached Spain, so far removed from the East and untouched by the Mongol invasions. Art formed a link between East and West, and even between the Nasrid Sultan of Granada and Timur himself, the scourge of the East and the builder of towers of skulls. The Nasrid sultans in their tiny kingdom fostered a miniature and delicate art; the world conqueror demanded art that was large and splendid, a fitting memorial to his mighty deeds. But both he and the sultans of Granada delighted in gardens, and both, in their own ways, were lovers of beautiful things. When Timur chose Samarkand to be the capital of his kingdom in Persia, he carried away there the finest artists and craftsmen from the cities he had conquered, and under the patronage of Timur and his sons, Persian artists were to excel themselves in the brilliance of their work.

SILK TEXTILE
Hispano-Moresque,
14th–15th century

ROYAL TOMBS AT
THE SHAH-I-ZANDAH,
SAMARKAND

peRSIA anδ the house of timuR

IN THE YEAR 1403 a Christian king of Spain, Henry III of Castile and León, sent an embassy to Timur, bearing messages of goodwill and costly gifts. The party was led by the Spanish ambassador, Ruy González de Clavijo, who kept a diary of the long journey, first by ship from Spain to Constantinople and then over mountains and deserts to Timur's wondrous city, Samarkand.

When they crossed the border between Turkey and Persia, the Spanish party met by chance the caravan of an ambassador from Egypt, also on his way to Samarkand. He too was laden with gifts, which included six ostriches and a giraffe, and the two ambassadors continued their eastward journey together.

Passing through Tabriz, the old Mongol capital, they found it partly in ruins but still prosperous, with silks, cottons, and perfumes for sale in the bazaar. Sultaniya, farther along their road, was bustling with merchants from Venice and Genoa, Turkey, Syria, and Trebizond, and caravan loads of Indian spices arrived there from the East every summer. Timur, like the Mongols before him, encouraged trade and travel in his kingdom, and as the ambassadors journeyed on through the deserts of northern Persia, they found in each town a posthouse where they could get fresh horses, free lodging, and food.

When they came to Meshed, "the chief place of pilgrimage in all these parts," the Spanish ambassador, although a Christian, was allowed to see the tomb of the Imam Reza within the magnificent shrine. "Any pilgrim who has been here," he remarked, "on returning home to his own country, his neighbors will come up to him and kiss the hem of his garment, for they hold that he has visited a very holy place."

Nearing Samarkand at last, after many days' travel across waterless deserts beyond Meshed, the ambassadors rejoiced to see the gardens, cotton fields, and orchards around the city. They found the streets of Samarkand thronged with people of all nations, faiths, and languages—Mongols from the steppes, turbaned Indians and Persians, Russians and Chinese. Camel caravans padded through the city with the soft ringing of bells, and bales of merchandise were unloaded in the courtyards of the many caravansaries. In the great bazaar, built at Timur's command, the shops displayed gleaming silks from China, six months' march away, leather and linen from Russia and Central Asia, Indian spices, and swords, armor and jewelry of the finest workmanship. The town was filled with the craftsmen gathered there by Timur. From Damascus he had brought silk weavers, potters, and glassworkers, and makers of armor and crossbows. From Turkey, after his victory over the Ottoman sultan, Timur had carried away masons and silversmiths and the all-important gunsmiths who could make the arquebus, the newest kind of weapon.

Timur was an old man with his great conquests behind him, but he was still planning further campaigns. After a lifetime spent in military camps and nomad tents, he preferred to live outside the city. One of his palaces was in a large orchard called Dilkusha, Heart's Ease, and here, in the open air before the portal of the palace, he received the ambassadors from Egypt and Spain.

"He was sitting on the ground," Clavijo says, "but upon a raised dais before which there was a fountain that threw up a column of water into the air backward, and in the basin of the fountain there were floating red apples."

Timur wore a cloak of plain silk and a tall white hat with a ruby in the crown. Seated on a silken mattress and cushions, he graciously accepted the ambassadors' gifts, and the scarlet cloth from Spain was immediately divided among his eight wives. He presented the envoys with gowns of gold embroidery and fine horses, and invited them to a great feast to be held in the Royal Camp outside the town.

The Spanish ambassador was amazed by the tents and furnishings of the Royal Camp. The circular tents with their domed tops were shaped like the round felt *yurts* of the Central Asian nomads, but all were made of silk. Timur gave audience in a silken pavilion striped in white, black, and yellow and lined with crimson tapestry. Beautiful carpets were spread, indoors and out, for the guests to sit on while they ate vast quantities of mutton and horseflesh and drank gallons of wine and *kumiss,* the favorite drink of fermented mare's milk. Even women were allowed to enjoy the festivities, and in the tent of Timur's chief wife, the Great Khanum, Clavijo noticed a masterpiece of goldsmith's work—a golden oak tree as high as a man. Its leaves were made of rubies, emeralds, turquoises, sapphires, and pearls, and among the branches were many little birds of gold and colored enamel.

The silks and carpets, the metalwork and the rich costumes of Timur and his court have disappeared long ago, but some of the buildings that adorned his capital city still stand today in Samarkand. Timur and his successors contributed some magnificent buildings to the group of domed tombs called the Shah-i-Zandah, which was the traditional place of burial for noble families and members of the royal house.

The Shah-i-Zandah stands high on a mound above the city. The tall domes make a thrilling silhouette against the sky; but to discover the full glory of the buildings, we must climb the stone steps up the mound. As we follow the path between the tombs, we see at last the splendor of their decoration. There is faïence mosaic in blue, black, white, and yellow, in angular geometric pat-

95

terns and free-swirling arabesques. Under the entrance archways the tiles are moulded into stalactites, each hollowed cell with a separate pattern in blue and white, while up the walls are bands of blue-glazed tiles in which the arabesques are deeply carved and the patterns outlined in black shadow.

· The tomb of Timur stands apart from the Shah-i-Zandah, a massive octagonal building crowned by a tall blue dome. It was finished at about the time of the ambassadors' visit and was intended to be a tomb for Timur's favorite grandson, Muhammad Sultan. The lines of the building are simple, adding to the sense of monumental size, and the decoration is simplified to austere geometric patterns of glazed bricks. Majestic Kufic lettering in black and white marches around the high cylindrical drum that supports the dome, and the amazing dome itself is ribbed from top to base with rounded ridges under the skin of shining tiles. Sunlight filters through openwork grilles in the drum to light the dome chamber within, where Timur's dark green tombstone stands out among the memorials to Muhammad Sultan and others of the royal house.

TIMUR'S TOMB, SAMARKAND

Timur died in 1404, soon after the departure of the ambassadors. His son Shah Rukh, who succeeded him, moved the capital to Herat in Khorasan, where he had been serving as governor. Shah Rukh set himself to repair the ruin left by his father's invasions, and his wife, Gauhar Shad, commanded the building of the great mosque that bears her name, in the precincts of the shrine at Meshed. Its huge turquoise dome can still be seen above the high walls of the shrine, and hidden within are tile decorations as rich as those at Samarkand.

The art of faïence mosaic reached its height in Persia in the fifteenth century, with Meshed and Isfahan as the two centers. This was art on a large scale, clothing whole buildings with spectacular beauty, but it also shows us the Persians' love of the miniature. The tilemakers covered walls and minarets with patterns that have all the delicacy of the illuminations on a page of manuscript, and the inscriptions woven into the designs were based on the elegant calligraphy of books.

This was the golden age of Persian bookmaking. The artists and craftsmen of the fifteenth century were never surpassed in calligraphy, illumination, and the making of beautiful book covers of cut and tooled leather. Above all, the painters of miniatures developed a true Persian style that was to set the pattern for generations of artists to come.

Timur's successors were the patrons of miniature painters. The great conqueror had no use for an art so small, and when he brought painters to Samarkand from the plundered cities of Shiraz and Baghdad, he probably set them to work on large murals glorifying his deeds and battles rather than on tiny pictures to be hidden between the pages of books. Some of the miniature painters of Shiraz and Baghdad must have escaped capture by Timur, for in both cities, at the end of the fourteenth century, a new and wonderful style of painting was born.

We have seen how Persian artists under the Mongols had been influenced by the art of China, especially in their rendering of animals and landscape. Now we find the Chinese qualities blended with the Persian love of pattern, color, and minute detail. The new style appears in all its loveliness in a miniature painted by an artist of Baghdad named Junaid, in 1396. His picture is one of seven illustrations for a romance in verse, the love story of a prince and princess. The garden where the hero and heroine are feasting among their courtiers is painted as though we were looking down on it from above. The horizon is set high at the top of the picture and the foreground at the bottom, and the

BOOK COVER:
OUTSIDE *(left)*
INSIDE, WITH
CUT-LEATHER
DECORATION
(right)
Persian, 15th century

earth is dotted with clumps of flowers. The slender graceful figures, brightly clad, overlap each other as they recede into the
background, but the whole effect is of flat surface pattern instead
of deep space.

99

BAHRAM GUR
HUNTING (*In this
version of the story
he shoots a wild ass,
not a gazelle*)
*From a manuscript
of poems by Nizami,
Herat, 15th century*

All the new elements in Junaid's picture became part of the language of the Persian painters who lived after him. Their pictures, like his, were filled with a gentle dreamy atmosphere. There were none of the strong emotions and wild expressive gestures that we saw in the mourning scene from the great *Shah Nama* of Tabriz. Their jewel-like art was relaxing and refreshing, designed to delight their princely patrons. The artists loved to paint the rich designs of carpets, tiles, and costumes and to put their figures against a background of trees and flowers, or in one of the formal Persian gardens so dear to them in a dry and barren land.

In a picture showing Bahram Gur's famous hunting expedition, the artist has made the desert itself look as neat as a garden, edged with bluish rocks and fantastic little trees. The picture is an illustration for a section of the *Khamsa*, a set of five narrative poems by the Persian poet Nizami. The manuscript was copied and illuminated for Baisunkur Mirza, the son of Shah Rukh. A gentle, pleasure-loving prince, delicate in health, Baisunkur

Mirza assembled at his palace in Herat forty of the finest painters in Persia to illustrate books for his library. Romantic poetry, such as the *Khamsa,* was favorite reading at his court, but his most famous book was an exquisite *Shah Nama,* completed in 1430.

Not all painters of the fifteenth century worked in the courtly style of Herat. This miniature, painted in Shiraz in 1480, is altogether more robust. It comes from a copy of the *Khavaran Nama,* which tells the story of Ali, the son-in-law of the Prophet Muhammad. The painter, who signed himself as "Farhad, the humblest of slaves," used brilliant colors. His figures are large, strong, and stocky, with big heads; and large trees and realistic green grasses fill the background of the picture.

This change of style in painting was due to a change of rulers in Shiraz. Throughout the early fifteenth century the "Black Sheep" and "White Sheep" Turkmans from northeastern Persia had been battling between themselves and against the successors of Timur, and by the mid-century they had conquered all of Timur's Persian kingdom except for Herat and the province of Khorasan. Shiraz fell to them in 1452, and under the new masters the artists of Shiraz gradually adopted the so-called Turkman style, blending it with the conventions of the Persian miniature.

THREE MEN
BEFORE A
PALACE
*Miniature by
Farhad for the
Khavaran-Nama
Shiraz, 1480
(See frontispiece)*

MAJNUN WATCHING
THE FIGHTING TRIBESMEN
Miniature by Bihzad
for Nizami's Khamsa
Herat, 1493

At about the time that Farhad finished his masterpiece in Shiraz, an artist of genius was painting his first pictures in Herat. His name was Bihzad, a name forever famous in the story of Persian painting.

Bihzad was born in 1440 and worked at the court of Sultan Husain Mirza, the last ruling prince of Timur's line. Herat was then as rich and beautiful as Timur's Samarkand, and Husain's gay court was dominated by poets and artists.

Bihzad was so famous in his lifetime that his name was often signed to pictures by other artists. This miniature, signed by Bihzad himself, was made for a copy of the *Khamsa* and illustrates the sad story of Majnun and Leila. A family feud prevented the lovers from marrying, and Majnun, desperate with grief, fled to the desert and became a hermit. Here he watches a battle in the desert between supporters of the rival families.

If we compare this picture with the one of Bahram Gur hunting, painted for the *Khamsa* of 1430, we can see where Bihzad's genius lay. His picture is filled with a new energy, drama, and realism. His people are more than graceful figures in a dreamlike landscape. The warriors and their camels are drawn as though from life in a vigorous circular composition, and their setting is a real desert, a pale barren background for the vivid green, blue, orange, and tawny yellow of the figures. In Bihzad's paintings we see people and animals as individuals—rich men and poor men, old and young, the elders in the mosque and the herdsmen camping among their horses in the fields.

Yet Bihzad never overstepped the limits of the miniature style. His desert scene has the same viewpoint, high horizon, and flat golden sky as the Bahram Gur picture. He was famous for battle paintings, and made handsome illustrations for a book of the deeds of Timur, in which he painted armor and weapons correct in every detail. But his battle scenes are beautiful patterns of movement and color, and show little of the ferocity of war, so bitterly familiar to the people of his time.

The fifteenth century brought war, unrest, and change not only to Persia but throughout the Near East. In Asia Minor the Ottoman Turks had quickly recovered from Timur's invasion and were carving out an ever-widening empire for themselves. Led by their sultan, Mehmet the Conqueror, they cut deep into the Byzantine Empire until the emperor held only the ancient city of Constantinople. In 1453, after weeks of siege by the Turks, the city fell. To the people of Western Europe, the fall of Constantinople seemed a catastrophe beyond imagination; to the Turks it was a crowning triumph. The Christian city of Constantinople became the Moslem capital, Istanbul, where the wealth of the Turkish sultans rivaled the vanished glory of Byzantium.

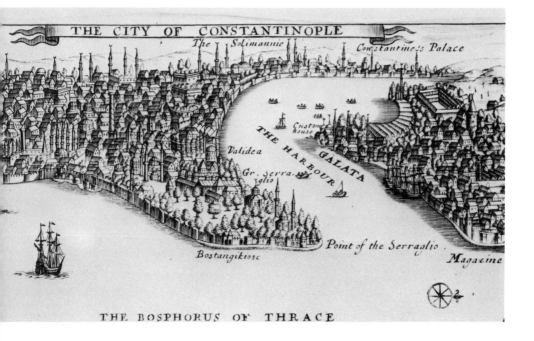

THE CITY OF CONSTANTINOPLE

The Solimanuie   *Constantine's Palace*

Custom house

Validea   THE HARBOUR   GALATA

Gr. Serra- glio

Bostangikiosc   *Point of the Serraglio.*

Magazine

THE BOSPHORUS OF THRACE

istanbul and the ottoman turks

BY THE MIDDLE of the sixteenth century the Ottoman sultan, Suleyman the Magnificent, was the most powerful ruler in the Moslem world. His empire extended over Turkey, Syria, and Iraq, as far as the Persian Gulf; he had conquered Egypt, destroying the last of the Mamluks; he controlled western Arabia and the holy cities of Mecca and Medina, and he had invaded the North African shore to the borders of Morocco. Turkish armies pressed far into Europe until they battered at the gates of Vienna. Turkish ships controlled the Mediterranean and the rich sea-going trade with the Far East across the Indian Ocean, and Turkish pirates were the terror of the seas from the English Channel to the coastal waters of India.

The heart of this mighty empire was the imperial capital, Istanbul, and travelers flocked there from East and West. The merchants, ambassadors, and adventurers of Western Europe might fear and hate the sultan—the Grand Turk as they called

VIEW OF ISTANBUL,
LOOKING WEST
Detail from a 17th-century engraving

him—but all who sailed to Istanbul were thrilled by the beauty of his capital. Many had endured weeks aboard ship in the Mediterranean, running the gauntlet of the Barbary pirates. They were thankful to slip into the shelter of the Sea of Marmara, and as their ships approached the narrower waters of the Bosporus, the goal of the long journey rose ahead like a vision.

The city crowned a hilly point of land, curving out from the western shore of the Sea of Marmara and forming the gateway to the Bosporus. The skyline was dominated by the domes and tall slender minarets of mosques. Between the buildings were thickets of green trees pricked by the sharp dark spears of cypresses; and at the northern tip of the point, where the Bosporus was joined by the Golden Horn, were the grim gray walls of the Seraglio, the huge and mysterious palace of the sultan.

Travelers were often disappointed by a closer view of the city when they disembarked among narrow muddy streets and mean wooden houses, but they could not fail to be impressed by the splendor and majesty of the mosques. The sultans and their ministers had built many mosques in Istanbul since the time of the conquest, but Suleyman the Magnificent, with the wealth of the empire at his disposal, was the greatest builder of all, and his Royal Architect, Sinan, was a man of genius.

Sinan had begun his career as a soldier in the sultan's army and served as military engineer and bridgebuilder. When he finally devoted himself to architecture, he designed and erected more than three hundred buildings in his long life. In 1550, at the sultan's command, he laid the foundations of the Suleymaniye Mosque on the third, and highest, of the city's seven hills. Thousands of workmen labored for seven years on the mosque and the buildings connected with it—religious schools, a medical college and hospital, a *han* and a bazaar. When at last the work was done, Sinan could say proudly to the sultan: "I have built for thee, O Emperor, a mosque that will remain on the face of the earth till the day of judgment. . . ."

Today, when we enter the courtyard of Sinan's mosque, our first impression is of the sheer size and power of the building.

THE SULEYMANIYE
MOSQUE, ISTANBUL

In contrast to the four sharply pointed minarets, the prayer hall
is a massive hill of masonry with the great dome as its summit
and the two half-domes and many small domes mounting up to it
like lesser peaks. In the hands of Turkish builders before Sinan,
the central dome had already become the main theme in the
architecture of mosques. Sinan was following the Ottoman and
Seljuk tradition when he designed his mosque as a domed prayer
hall facing an open arcaded courtyard, but he also studied the
greatest Byzantine building in Istanbul, Hagia Sophia, the
Church of the Holy Wisdom. Built in the sixth century by the
Emperor Justinian and turned into a mosque by Mehmet the
Conqueror, Hagia Sophia was famous for its miraculous dome,
which seemed to be suspended over the vast central space of the
interior.

In the Suleymaniye Mosque Sinan achieved an even greater
sense of space. As soon as we pass through the door, our eyes
are drawn upward to the soaring height of the dome that seems
even loftier than that of Hagia Sophia. Supporting it are the two
half-domes to the north and south, while the space below is extended to east and west to form broad open aisles for the lines

of worshipers. There are no dark mysterious corners in the building, as in Hagia Sophia. Light pours in through many windows, some of them filled with beautiful stained glass. Sinan, like other Turkish builders, must have had in his mind the verse from the Koran: "God is the light of the Heavens and the earth."

In 1560, when his masterpiece was finished, Sinan was at work on a much smaller mosque, which bears the name of Rustem Pasha, the sultan's son-in-law and grand vizier. Instead of standing proudly on a hilltop, the Rustem Pasha Mosque is down among the markets and docks by the busy waterway of the Golden Horn, which divides the old Turkish city from the foreign settlements of Galata and Pera. A flight of stone steps leads up from the street to a small courtyard above the bustle of the bazaars below. Along the front of the prayer hall is a porch, roofed with five small domes, and the wall in its shadow is decorated with panels and niches of brilliantly painted tiles, a foretaste of what we shall see within. The simple spacious interior is surmounted by a central dome and four small half-domes, with a low vaulted aisle on either side, but it is the decoration rather than the architecture that makes the building so beautiful.

The walls and the piers that support the dome are covered with tiles—a garden of wonderful floral designs painted in turquoise, dark blue, and rich tomato-red on a white ground. In

107

TILE DESIGN
*From the Rustem
Pasha Mosque*

TURKISH POTTERY:
Above JUG PAINTED
IN BLUE, PURPLE AND
GREEN *About 1540–50*
Below DISH PAINTED
IN BLUE AND TURQUOISE
About 1530

the large panels of the porch the square tiles are fitted together to make complete pictures, such as a flowering plum tree among tulips, carnations, and lilies. Inside, we find smaller, repeating patterns of flowers and leaves and interlacing stems, while in the *mihrab* the flowers are enclosed in a vase-shaped medallion. Everywhere we see the pointed shape of the budding tulip, for the tulip was the favorite flower of the Turks. It grew wild in Central Asia, and the Seljuks had brought tulips with them to Asia Minor. There are said to be forty-one different tulip patterns in the Rustem Pasha Mosque.

The art of the Turkish potters and tilemakers was at its best when this beautiful mosque was built and decorated. The old techniques of gold luster and faïence mosaic had been discarded in favor of square tiles painted in bright colors and covered with a clear glaze. Both pottery and tiles were made in the workshops of Isnik, not far from Istanbul. Bowls and dishes, jugs and mosque lamps were painted with the same vigorous floral designs as the tiles, at first only in shades of blue, in imitation of Chinese blue-and-white porcelain, but later in turquoise, purple, green, black, and red.

Tiles made at Isnik adorned the houses of the Turkish nobility and the palace of the sultan. Today, in the Seraglio, we can see rooms lined with

108

tiles from floor to ceiling, but for centuries all this beauty was hidden from the world. Most of the palace was closed to everyone but the people who lived there, and outsiders could only speculate about the wonders within.

Mehmet the Conqueror began the building of the Seraglio, and by the time of Suleyman the Magnificent the palace had grown to the size of a small town, and hundreds of the inhabitants never went beyond the Imperial Gate in the high gray walls. Inside this gate was the first courtyard, a broad park that was open to everyone and usually crowded with people. A road led through the park to the second gate, the Gate of Peace, where envoys to the sultan had to dismount from their horses. No one might ride beyond this point, and no one was admitted to the second courtyard except on business. The Gate of Peace was also the place of execution, and it could not have been reassuring to visitors to see the heads of offenders prominently displayed there.

Those who entered the second courtyard were oppressed by the strange silence. Soldiers, servants, gardeners, and ministers of state all went about their business without speaking, for any noise might disturb the sultan. Down the right-hand side of the court were the royal kitchens, and to the left the Hall of the Divan where the sultan's ministers met and where ambassadors were received by the grand vizier. They were generally served a lavish dinner before being conducted through the Gate

109

TILE DESIGN
*From the Rustem
Pasha Mosque*

of Felicity at the far end of the court and into the Throne Room beyond. There they were permitted to see the sultan, sitting silent upon a jeweled throne, half hidden by his courtiers. They could say no word to him directly, but only through the vizier, and before backing away across the carpeted floor, they were expected to bow low and kiss the hem of the sultan's robe.

Behind the Throne Room was the Enderun, the Interior, where no visitor could go. To the left of the third courtyard, which contained the sultan's library and a mosque, was the vast labyrinth of buildings occupied by the sultan and his harem, the royal princes and multitudes of slaves. The fourth courtyard was a garden, reaching to the tip of Seraglio Point, where successive rulers built kiosks, or small pavilions, in which to take their ease while looking out over the blue waters of the Bosporus and the Golden Horn.

Although visitors could see little of the palace, they were dazzled by the costumes of its inhabitants. Some of the beautiful clothes worn by the sultans and their retainers have come down to us today. A brocade gown that belonged to Sultan Bayezid II, early in the sixteenth century, is covered with swirling leaves and flowers in red, pink, green, and blue against a white background, like the designs of tiles and pottery. Mehmet the Conqueror wore a gown adorned with "tiger stripes and leopard spots," a design brought from Central Asia and specially associated with royalty, for the three circles were the badge of Timur. We also find fabrics with patterns of flames, and with the crescents and stars that were the symbols of Christian Constantinople before the conquest; but most of the materials were like blossoming gardens, with the tulip always the favorite flower.

Turkish silks and velvets had been famous in Europe since the fourteenth century. Many fabrics were designed with patterns suited to Italian taste and sold to the Genoese merchants who lived at Galata, across the Golden Horn. The Italians also ran a brisk trade in Turkish carpets, which were so highly prized in

TURKISH
TEXTILE DESIGNS

WOOLEN PILE RUG
Turkish,
16th–17th century

Europe that they were used as table-cloths rather than as covers for the floor. In 1521 Cardinal Wolsey in England ordered through Venetian merchants no less than sixty carpets from Turkey for his palace at Hampton Court, and Turkish carpets often appear in the paintings of German, Flemish, and Italian artists of this period.

The Ottoman carpet weavers used the same technique and bright colors as the Seljuks, but the geometric patterns of their rugs were more complicated, and the Kufic script in the borders was replaced by angular arabesques. The carpets made in Ushak in Anatolia were particularly varied in design. Some have floral patterns, reminding us of the tiles; some, the stripes and spots we saw on the Conqueror's robe; and others, the medallion design that originated in Persia. Ushak carpets were much in demand in Europe, and noblemen often had them made to order and blazoned with their coats of arms.

TURKISH TEXTILE DESIGNS
OF THE 16TH CENTURY:
Top VELVET IN ITALIAN STYLE
Below SILK AND GOLD TISSUE

111

TUGHRA OF
SULEYMAN THE
MAGNIFICENT
1520–66

The finest Turkish carpets were those made for use in the palace. In these the floral patterns were too involved and detailed to be worked with the "Turkish knot." The weavers adopted the type of knot used by the Persians, in which the tufted ends of the thread lay closer together and formed a more velvety pile. Among the palace carpets were prayer rugs, large enough for one person to kneel on. Prayer rugs differed in design from other carpets. The center of the rug was usually filled by a shape representing a *mihrab*. In the large prayer rug shown on page 115, the niche is divided into three parts, with flowers sprouting at the bottom and a mosque lamp hanging in the middle.

PERSIAN
KNOT

The palace was a center for craftsmen of all kinds, from leatherworkers and makers of weapons to jewelers and embroiderers, and it was traditional for the sultans themselves to be skilled in crafts. Some of them were excellent calligraphers, and we can still see today their sets of pens and tiny ivory-handled penknives. Calligraphy was a highly respected art in Turkey. Whenever the sultan issued a *firman*, or written decree, his monogram—the *Tughra*—appeared at the head of the document. The monogram was always a masterpiece of calligraphy, beautifully illuminated, as we see in the *Tughra* of Suleyman the Magnificent, which is filled with tiny flowers.

Suleyman employed calligraphers to copy books for his library and painters to make the illustrations. This fine miniature, typical of the work of the Turkish court painters, comes from a book on the military campaigns of Sultan Bayezid II. Here he attacks the Byzantine army, fighting single-handed against their leader. Be-

hind the sultan the Turkish troops march down from a fortress
on a rocky height, and in the foreground they pursue the fleeing
enemy and take one man prisoner.

The design of the composition, with its high horizon and
strong sense of pattern, reveals the influence of Persian miniature
painters, some of whom came to work in Istanbul in the sixteenth

113

HORSERACE
Detail from
miniature by Osman
in the Hunername

century; but Turkish artists, like the painter of this picture, worked on a larger scale than the Persians, their technique was broader and bolder and their subjects quite different. The Persian painters, as we have seen, usually illustrated the heroic legends of the *Shah Nama* and pictured the dream-world of romantic poetry. The Turkish artists were called upon to paint portraits and to record historical events. Their pictures told stories in a simple direct style, sometimes with deep feeling and often with a touch of humor.

One of the best-known historical painters was Osman, who worked for Suleyman the Magnificent. Between 1550 and 1590 Osman illustrated two great volumes, called the *Hunername*, recounting the history of the Ottoman sultans and particularly the life and campaigns of Suleyman himself. In large compositions with scores of gaily-colored figures Osman shows us the sultan's army on the march, charging into battle and besieging a city. We also find peaceful scenes of country life and sport, including a vivid picture of a horse race on a day of festival, in which brown, fawn and pale-blue horses gallop at full stretch over the lilac-colored ground.

Weddings and other joyful events in the sultan's household were always celebrated by festivals in Istanbul, and Osman illustrated an entire book, the *Surname*, as a record of the processions on one of these great days. Men of the various crafts and trades of city and country passed in review before the sultan, and Osman painted them all, from street-sweepers and taxidermists to shepherds with lively sheep and goats.

Osman's pictures are like windows through which we see the life of his time. The Turkish painters who worked for the Ottoman

PRAYER RUG
Turkish,
17th century

sultans were the reporters and photographers of their day, and
sometimes traveled with the sultan's armies, in order to record
on the spot the great victories and conquests.

All through the sixteenth century the sultans tried to extend
their empire eastward into Persia, but here even Suleyman the
Magnificent met his match. The fighting swayed to and fro along
the border, but the Persians were united against him and fired
by a flaming patriotism. Out of the wreck of the empire of Timur
and the wars between the Turkman tribes a new dynasty had
arisen at the end of the fifteenth century, the first truly Persian
dynasty to rule the country since the Arab invasion. Shah Ismail,
the first of the Safavid line, united the country under his rule
and re-established the capital at Tabriz, and when his son
Tahmasp succeeded him in 1524, the stage was set for a wonderful revival of Persian art.

SHEPHERDS
Detail from a ·
miniature by Osman
in the Surname

peRsia and the safavid shahs

WHEN THE YOUNG Shah Tahmasp came to the throne of Persia, he was an enthusiastic amateur painter and a personal friend of his court artist and teacher, Sultan Muhammad. The court at Tabriz had become a center for painting and bookmaking since the conquest of Herat in 1507 by the Uzbegs, a tribe from Central Asia. The great Bihzad himself had come from Herat to Tabriz, and Shah Ismail had made him head of the Royal Library and supervisor of painters, calligraphers, bookbinders and all the craftsmen involved in the making of sumptuous books.

Bihzad died at the beginning of Tahmasp's reign, but the young shah inherited the Royal Library with its staff of skilled painters, most of them pupils and followers of the old master. Among the first books they made for Tahmasp was a beautiful manuscript of Nizami's *Khamsa,* containing an illustration that might serve as a picture of the young shah and his court. It shows the Persian hero Khusrau enthroned among his courtiers in a paved garden, an embroidered canopy over his head and a fine carpet spread beneath the throne. The figures, slender and graceful in the style of Bihzad, wear the rich costumes of the Safavid

116

court, and their white turbans are wound around a long projecting
stick, a fashion peculiar to Tahmasp's reign.

Nizami's poems, ever popular at court, were copied again
for the shah's library in the years between 1539 and 1543, and
one of the illustrations for this magnificent book was painted by
Tahmasp's friend Sultan Muhammad. It shows an episode that
had long been a favorite subject for artists. Khusrau, riding

KHUSRAU AND
SHIRIN *From a
manuscript of
Nizami's Khamsa
1539–43*

through the wilderness, sees by chance the beautiful Shirin
bathing in a wayside pool. The two are already in love, and
Shirin, disguised as a man, has journeyed to Persia in search of
the young prince.

The arrangement of the two figures in the picture follows a
long-standing tradition, but Sultan Muhammad has set them in

a lovely landscape of his own invention. The fantastic rocks around Shirin's pool are in shades of lavender, sea-green, and sandy lion color, and her swift black horse, Shabdiz, prances on green grass sown with flowers. Shirin's clothes are draped over a pink-blossoming fruit tree, and against the golden sky above, with its little scrolled Chinese clouds, stands a tall chenar, the oriental plane tree so beloved in Persia. As though the miniature alone were not rich enough, the broad margin of the page is painted in gold with deer and foxes among leafy flowering plants.

For manuscripts as sumptuous as this *Khamsa*, the painters designed exquisite covers, patterned with flowers, birds, and landscapes. The covers were ornamented inside and out, and also on the flap that folded over the front edges of the book. Tahmasp's bookbinders used the same techniques of leatherwork as the craftsmen of Herat in the fifteenth century—gold tooling, embossing, and cutting designs in openwork. For still finer detail, they cut out paper filigree for the linings of the covers, and prepared bindings of leather and papier-mâché with a smooth coating of lacquer on which the artists could paint miniatures in water color. A single painted cover would take months of patient work with tiny brushes of kitten's hair.

BOOK COVER WITH PRESSED AND GILDED DECORATION
Persian, 16th century

The painters who designed book covers were also called upon to make patterns for carpets, like those they portrayed with such loving care in their miniatures. Carpets had been woven by the nomads and villagers of Persia long before the country was conquered by the Arabs, and the Safavid shahs, as the first native rulers for centuries, were glad to encourage such a typically Persian craft. The weavers already had the skill born of generations of experience, and most of them used the "Persian knot" that produced carpets of a fine velvet texture. All they needed were the new designs that the court artists could provide. Shah Tahmasp probably established a carpet factory at his palace, and he even designed carpets himself. In spite of the constant strife with Turkey, he wrote to Suleyman the Magnificent, offering to have a set of carpets made for the newly finished Suleymaniye Mosque, and the offer was gladly accepted.

Some of the most glorious Persian carpets were made for mosques and shrines, and of these the Ardebil carpet is the acknowledged masterpiece. It was an offering to the shrine of Sheik Safi, the saintly ancestor of the Safavid shahs, who was buried in the tomb mosque at Ardebil in northwestern Persia. The dark blue ground of the carpet, like a Paradise garden, is thickly covered with flowers and twining stems. In the center is a great golden medallion with smaller medallions radiating from it, and two hanging mosque lamps, symbolic of the carpet's sacred use. A quarter of the centerpiece is placed in each of the four corners, and the dark purple border is filled with flowers and small panels of arabesques in red, green, and yellow. Although the detail is so rich, the balance and stillness of the design give a feeling of peace and meditation.

The Ardebil carpet is one of the very few to be signed and dated by its creator: "The work of the slave of the threshold, Maqsud of Kashan, in the year 946 (1540)." Perhaps Maqsud was both the designer and the weaver. His town, Kashan, was famous for textile crafts as well as for pottery and tiles, and it is thought to be the place where silk carpets were made.

Most carpets were woven of wool, sometimes mixed with gold

THE ARDEBIL
CARPET
Persian, 1540

and silver threads, but for court use or as gifts to foreign princes the shah demanded rugs entirely of silk. Like the Ardebil carpet, this small silk rug is designed around a central medallion, but the whole effect is more restless and lively. The dark blue medallion is patterned in green and silver; brightly colored flowers and Chinese cloud bands are dotted over the surrounding field of deep red, and the border is black and blue-green. Another silk rug has an all-over pattern of animals, running, fighting, and chasing one another on a flowery ground.

These two popular designs—medallions and animals—were sometimes combined with splendid effect, as we can see in a fragment from a woolen carpet probably made at Ardebil at the same time as Maqsud's masterpiece. Figures of people might also be introduced into the central medallion, while in the marvelous "Hunting Carpets" the whole field was covered with lively figures of horsemen and fleeing animals.

The Persian rugs that were probably best known in Europe were the floral carpets of Herat, which we recognize in Dutch and Spanish paintings of the sixteenth and seventeenth centuries. By this time more European travelers were finding their way to Persia, bringing back Persian goods and telling strange tales of the wonders they had seen in a land that still seemed as remote as the world of the *Arabian Nights.*

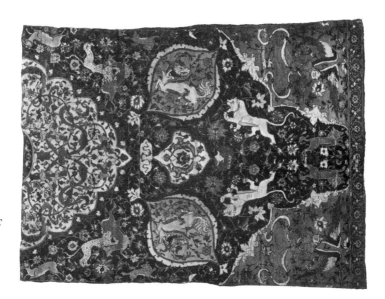

PART OF A
WOOLEN CARPET
Persian,
16th century

The pioneers were hardheaded Italian merchants who had long been active in the silk trade. Persian silks, brocades, and velvets were highly prized in Europe. They were often made up into church vestments, even when their designs were distinctly unsuitable. The Persians were fond of floral patterns, but they had no scruples about weaving the figures of animals and people into their fabrics. The silk weavers were as skilled as the makers of carpets, and the court painters were ready with designs as delicate as miniatures in manuscripts. A young warrior leading a Turkish captive through the forest; an elegant youth in a garden with bottle and winecup in hand; or the familiar story of Khusrau and Shirin—all were woven into silks and velvets to be worn by the high dignitaries of Tahmasp's court or presented as gifts to foreign ambassadors.

Merchants of other nations were not slow to compete with the Italians in the race for the Persian trade. The first Englishmen arrived at the court of Shah Tahmasp in the mid-sixteenth century when the shah had moved his capital eastward to Kazvin, out of danger of Turkish attack. After a long and harrowing journey from Russia, the Englishmen were coldly received. The shah was no longer a gay, artistic youth but a harsh fanatical man who would make no trade agreement with Christians.

Though he later grew more friendly toward Europeans, it was his successor, Shah Abbas I, who welcomed Western visitors.

Thomas Herbert, a young man who accompanied the English ambassador to Persia in 1627, summed up Shah Abbas' character: "Whom he loves, the King honours; such as he hates, the King crushes all to pieces." Warrior, administrator, and patron of the arts, Shah Abbas was rightly called The Great. His reign marks the height of Safavid power and glory. He fought off the Turks; he built roads and caravansaries for the safety of travelers, and palaces and gardens for himself; but his supreme achievement was the building of Isfahan.

Shah Abbas decided in 1598 to move his capital from Kazvin to Isfahan, the old capital of Persia under the Seljuk Turks. As we have seen, the town of Isfahan centered upon the Friday Mosque and the sultan's palace. Shah Abbas built his new town southwest of the old one, but it was not a walled palace-city for the court and government alone. The main market place and the old bazaars were all part of his plan; his palaces, mosques, and gardens adjoined the houses and shops of the people.

The heart of the new Isfahan was the great square, the Maidan-e-Shah, which Thomas Herbert described as "without doubt as spacious, as pleasant and aromatic a market as any in the universe." A huge rectangle, almost a third of a mile in length, the Maidan served not only as a market but as a polo ground or an arena for wild-beast shows and archery contests. The stone goal posts for polo still stand at the ends of the Maidan, and except for the public garden in the center, the great square appears to us today as it did to Thomas Herbert more than three

ISFAHAN:

THE MAIDAN, LOOKING SOUTH

TO THE SHAH'S MOSQUE

centuries ago. As we gaze in wonder at the vastness and majesty of its plan, we can understand the old proud saying of the Isfahanis: *"Isfahan nisf-e-jahan"*—Isfahan is half the world.

The Maidan is bounded on all four sides by a two-story façade with arched shopfronts below and decorative pointed arches above. Many of the shops belong to metalworkers who still make engraved trays and vessels of copper and silver as their ancestors did in Thomas Herbert's time. At the north end of the square the line of shops is broken by the monumental arched entrance of the bazaar, leading into a network of covered streets under lofty churchlike vaults.

As we walk down the long eastern side of the Maidan, we come to the fawn-colored dome and exquisite blue façade of the Sheik Lutfullah Mosque, built by Shah Abbas in 1603 in memory of his father-in-law. The mosque is small and simple, consisting only of the entrance archway and a passage opening into the square chamber below the dome, but the wonderful faïence mosaic, covering the walls and dome, makes it one of the loveliest buildings in all Persian architecture. On the dome are bold arabesques of stems, leaves, and flowers spreading over the fawn-colored background, patterns large enough to be seen from the other side of the Maidan. The decorations inside are miniature in their delicacy. The dome is lined with medallions radiating from a

ISFAHAN:
ENTRANCE OF
THE SHAH'S MOSQUE

centerpiece of curling arabesques—the medallion carpet design miraculously translated into faïence mosaic. Arabic inscriptions stand out in white against bands of dark blue, and around the arches are ropelike blue moldings of shining ceramic.

In contrast to the delicacy of the Sheik Lutfullah Mosque is the massive Shah's Mosque whose lofty entrance *iwan* and twin minarets dominate the southern end of the Maidan. Like the old Friday Mosque, the building is planned around a central court; but the court and the prayer hall with its great blue dome are set at an angle behind the arched entrance, in order to point southwest toward Mecca. Even here, the vast spaces of the walls, dome, and minarets are covered with tiles. So many tiles were needed and the shah was in such a hurry to finish the work that square tiles, glazed and painted, were used as well as faïence mosaic. The workmanship is not so fine as in the smaller mosque, but the building gives an overwhelming impression of majesty and richness.

As we turn along the western side of the Maidan, we come to the Ali Kapu, the Lofty Gate of the palace grounds. Six stories high, the building has a pillared veranda on the fourth floor which the shah used as a grandstand for watching games and festivities and as a place for royal audiences and the reception of

ISFAHAN:
ALI KAPU

ambassadors. Thomas Herbert tells us that the rooms of the Ali
Kapu had ceilings of embossed plaster painted in red, blue, white,
and gold. We can still see today the mural paintings of courtiers
and their European guests, and the rooms with specially shaped
niches in the walls for the display of Chinese porcelain.

Behind the Ali Kapu was "the garden or wilderness . . . made
fragrant with flowers, filled with airy citizens privileged from
hurt or affrights. . . ." Only one building remains today of the
royal palaces and pavilions that were set about in these lovely
grounds. This is the Chehel Sotun, the Forty Pillars, which takes
its name from the twenty tall columns of its porch and their
twenty reflections in the long pool in front of the building. In
spite of its size, the Chehel Sotun has the lightness and gaiety
of a summerhouse, a proper setting for the torchlight parties that
delighted the shah and his court. The atmosphere of the surrounding garden, with its slender white chenar trees and green
lawns, is carried into the rooms within. The walls are painted
with garden scenes, and formerly there were beautiful doors
decorated with birds and flowers.

ISFAHAN:
CHEHEL SOTUN

PERSIAN TEXTILES:
Above SILK BROCADE
OF LEILA AND MAJNUN
Late 16th century
Below SILK VELVET
About 1600

Shah Abbas kept a large staff of artists and craftsmen busy in the palace workshops, near the royal stables for a thousand horses. Carpet weavers continued to work in the tradition of Shah Tahmasp's craftsmen, while the fabrics made for draperies and court costumes were richer than ever before.

A fabric with a complicated design might be made up of two or three silken cloths of different colors woven at the same time, one behind the other, each color being brought to the front of the material as it was needed in the pattern. Cloths of red and white, with the addition of silver thread, were used in a design showing the unfortunate lovers, Majnun and Leila, meeting in the wilderness. This silk was probably woven at Yazd, a desert town east of Isfahan, famous for its weavers. Fine velvets were made in both towns, varying in design from comparatively simple patterns of flowers and butterflies to figures in landscapes. A luxurious velvet, showing two young men in a garden against a background of cloth of gold, reflects the large-figure style of the seventeenth-century miniature painters. This style became popular in the later years of Shah Tahmasp's reign, when the shah had lost interest in expensive illustrated books, and his artists took to making single miniatures—scenes of country life, and portraits of courtiers, ladies, poets, and holy men.

MAN SEWING
*Drawing by
Riza-i-Abbasi
Early 17th
century*

ANIMALS
*From a silk tissue,
Persian, 16th century*

Though Shah Abbas' artists followed the same fashion, they still produced illustrated manuscripts. In 1614 they completed an extraordinary copy of the *Shah Nama*, illustrated in the brilliant style of the fifteenth century miniature painters. The splendid pictures were inspired by those in the famous *Shah Nama* of 1430, made for Baisunkur Mirza at Herat, and show the same exquisite colors and rich designs.

MAN SEWING
*Drawing by
Riza-i-Abbasi
Early 17th
century*

Riza-i-Abbasi was the greatest artist at Shah Abbas' court, and his rather languid figure drawings, with their rhythmic curving line, set a pattern for the mural painters and the designers of tiles. On page 130 is a typical panel of painted tiles showing a garden party, complete with a European visitor in a plumed hat. This panel, and many others like it, decorated the garden pavilions along the Chahar Bagh, the noble promenade that formed the eastern boundary of the palace grounds.

The Chahar Bagh, the Four Gardens, was planted with chenar trees and poplars, roses and jasmine, and five watercourses ran down it to join the river, the Zaindeh Rud, with pools and fountains along the way. On either side were gardens with walls of latticework and with little pavilions built over the entrance gates so that the ladies could watch the comings and goings of royal processions, hunting parties, and visiting ambassadors. The Chahar Bagh was planned as the splendid approach to the city. It crossed the river by a handsome bridge and led out to the Hazar Jerib, the Thousand Acres, a huge royal estate that was made into a garden by one of Shah Abbas' successors.

Shah Abbas died in 1628, and in the words of Sir John Chardin, a seventeenth century traveler: "When this Great Prince ceased to live, Persia ceased to prosper." Later Safavid shahs continued to beautify the capital, though the age of the finest buildings, manuscripts, carpets, and textiles was gone. Persian art declined in its own country, but its influence had already spread to enrich the art of distant lands, from Ottoman Turkey to India.

When we look eastward to India, we find that Persian ideas in art were carried there in the van of a conquering army. Shah Tahmasp had barely come to the throne when the forces of Babur, Prince of Kabul, set out from Afghanistan, bent on the conquest of India. Babur was a descendant of Timur. A warrior and a lover of art, he had seen the glorious buildings of Samarkand and savored the rich Persian culture of Herat. When he crushed the warring Muhammadan kingdoms planted in India by the Turks, he laid the foundations of a mighty united empire where the arts of India and Persia were to be fused together to produce the exciting new art of the Mughals.

DETAIL OF A TILE PANEL
From the Chahar Bagh, Isfahan, 1600–50

inòia anò the gReat muGhals—1

BABUR'S ARMY invaded India in the cold winter of 1525. The following spring, at the Battle of Panipat, his swift Mongol horsemen and Turkish artillery faced the forces of the Sultan of Delhi and scattered them like leaves in the wind. The victors marched on, unopposed, to occupy the cities of Delhi and Agra and to break open the sultan's fantastic treasuries of silver, gold, and gems. Babur took nothing for himself, and at Agra, when he had divided the loot among his faithful followers, he celebrated the victory by making a garden.

It was a Persian garden, such as Babur had known at Herat, Kabul, and Samarkand. He ordered a well to be dug to supply the garden with plentiful water, and in the manner of Moslem rulers everywhere, he built an audience chamber overlooking a reflecting pool. The grounds were then planted with flowers. "In every corner I planted suitable gardens," Babur says in his autobiography; "in every garden I sowed roses and narcissus regularly, in beds corresponding to each other."

Babur died in 1530, worn out with fighting to hold and enlarge his Indian kingdom. He had made himself the first of the Mughal emperors, but he was homesick for Afghanistan to the end, and was buried, at his own request, in a garden outside Kabul. With

MUSICIANS AT THE BIRTH OF SALIM
Detail of a miniature from the Akbar-Nama
Early 17th century (see page 136)

little time for the patronage of art, he was a keen collector of
Persian paintings, especially those by Bihzad and the artists of
Herat. His son Humayun, who succeeded him, inherited Babur's

MAJNUN BROUGHT TO LEILA'S CAMP

From a manuscript of Nizami's Khamsa, 1539–43

love of art but not his skill in war. Deposed by a rival chieftain, Humayun fled to Persia in 1543 and took refuge at the court of Shah Tahmasp at Kazvin.

There, among the beautiful books made for the shah's Royal Library, he must have seen the famous copy of the *Khamsa*, finished in 1543, and admired this lovely illustration of a scene from the story of Majnun and Leila. The painter of the picture, Mir Sayyid Ali, was a close follower of Bihzad, and Humayun liked his work so much that when the exiled emperor returned at last to his throne in India, he took the painter with him, together with a younger artist, Abdus Samad. These two became the founders of what we know as the Mughal school of painting.

Under the direction of Mir Sayyid Ali, whom Humayun honored with the title of "Marvel of the Realm," fifty Indian artists were employed at Agra on the illustrations for a long Persian romance about an uncle of the Prophet Muhammad, Amir Hamza. There were to be no less than fourteen hundred large pictures, painted on cotton cloth, for the twelve volumes of the story. Humayun died in 1556, long before the pictures were finished, but the work was carried on in the reign of his son Akbar, who was as fond of art as his father. Akbar could neither read nor write, but he loved to have books read to him and could recite by heart the fantastic tales of Amir Hamza.

The picture of an army attacking a town, shown on page 135, is one of many illustrations painted by Akbar's Indian artists for the *Amir Hamza*. Although they worked under Persian direction, the artists had a style of their own that was rooted in the ancient heritage of Indian painting. Comparing this picture with Mir Sayyid Ali's miniature from the *Khamsa*, we see at once the likeness between them. In both paintings the horizon is high, so that we seem to be surveying the action from above, while foreground and background are divided by a diagonal line of rocks with a tree at the top and bottom. But the differences between the paintings are equally plain. In the Persian painting the figures are small and delicate, with gentle, masklike faces. The Indian figures, crowded together, are robust, solid-looking, and boldly individualized. The Persian picture is dreamlike and calm; the Indian one is filled with violent energy and has the concrete reality of a historical scene. Even the tents of the military camp are realistically drawn, while the Persian tents are decorative shapes in a flat pattern.

Of the many books illustrated for Akbar, one of the most important was the *Akbar-Nama,* the story of his life and deeds. Akbar was the greatest of the Mughal emperors. By the beginning of the seventeenth century he ruled an empire covering the whole of northern India from the delta of the Ganges westward to Sind and Baluchistan. He was not only a warrior, constantly fighting to extend his realm, but a statesman who gave his people a wise and stable government, and a deep thinker who tried to resolve the religious differences between Moslems and Hindus.

The miniatures of the *Akbar-Nama* reflect the many sides of his character. We see him on pilgrimages to holy shrines; charging into battle in gilded armor, or hunting stampedes of fleeing animals. Some of the illustrations show the influence of Western art. In a joyful picture of the celebrations at the birth of Akbar's son Salim we can trace the European influence in the painting of the drapery, in the perspective of the buildings and courtyards of the palace, and in the little landscape at the top, with its misty green distance. Akbar, like Shah Abbas in Persia, welcomed Europeans to his court, and his interest in religion prompted him to invite Jesuit missionaries from the Portuguese settlement of Goa on India's west coast. The Jesuit fathers gave him a great illustrated Bible, printed in Antwerp by Christopher Plantin, and also paintings of the Virgin and Child, which Akbar's artists copied at the emperor's command.

Rumors of the legendary magnificence of the "Great Moghul" reached as far as England, and in 1585 three Englishmen arrived at Akbar's palace-city of Fathpur-Sikri near Agra. They were the survivors of a party of merchants who had set out for India two years before, bearing letters to the "Great Moghul" from Queen Elizabeth I.

"Agra and Fatepore are two very great Cities," wrote Ralph

Fitch, one of the three adventurers, "either of them greater than London, and very populous. . . . Hither is a great resort of Merchants from Persia, and out of India, and very much Merchandize of Silke and Cloth, and of precious Stones, both Rubies, Diamants, and Pearles."

SURPRISE ATTACK BY NIGHT
Illustration from the
Romance of Amir Hamza
1556–1575

Ralph Fitch and his companions were privileged to see Fathpur-Sikri in all its glory. Akbar commanded the building of the palace-city in 1569, and it was almost finished within ten years. Today, deserted and partly ruined, it remains one of the wonders of Indian architecture.

Coming to Fathpur-Sikri from Agra, twenty-three miles away, the three Englishmen saw before them the domes, cupolas, and rooftops of the palace, all built of red sandstone. In the court-yard in front of the Diwan-i-Am, the Public Audience Chamber, they joined the gaily-colored crowds of Indians, Persians, and Turks waiting for Akbar to appear, and watched in the streets of the city some of the emperor's "one thousand Elephants" and "thirtie thousand horses" and "such store of Ounces [leopards], Tygres, Buffles, Cockes and Hawkes, that is very strange to see."

The palaces and courtyards behind the Diwan-i-Am were forbidden to outsiders, but the Friday Mosque, the largest building in the city, was open to all. Its great southern entrance was the Buland Darwaza, the Triumphal Gate, which was built by Akbar to celebrate a victory and still stands today. The huge

FATHPUR-SIKRI:
THE BULAND DARWAZA

façade of red sandstone and white marble rises at the head of a steep flight of steps. The cupolas along the top are purely Indian in style, but the lofty arched recess in the center is a Persian *iwan* on a grand scale. As we pass into its shadow, we find the inner side of the gate scaled down in height to harmonize with the arcades around the court of the mosque.

Within this vast court is the small domed tomb of the saint, Salim Chisti, who foretold the birth of Akbar's son, Salim. The saint died in 1571, and the mosque was built in his honor. The great prayer hall with its three domes stands at the west end of the court; at the opposite end is the tall archway of the King's Gate, which was used daily by Akbar at the hours of prayer.

The mosque may remind us of buildings in other Moslem countries to the west, but the palaces of Fathpur-Sikri are more peculiarly Indian in their decoration and design. Their walls are adorned with rich relief carving; upper stories are converted into airy open verandas, and the wide jutting eaves of the roofs are supported by wonderfully sculptured brackets. The jewel-like house built by Akbar for his Christian wife, Miriam, overlooks a courtyard that was the heart of the palace quarter. Nearby is the Panch Mahal, a curious tower with five stories of

FATHPUR-SIKRI:
THE DIWAN-I-KHAS

open porches, but by far the most unusual building is the Diwan-i-Khas, the Private Audience Chamber. Built according to Akbar's own suggestions, it has a single room within, and in the center is a heavy octagonal pillar. At the top of the pillar three tiers of richly carved brackets, like the spreading branches of some strange tree, support a circular stone platform ten feet across at the level of the second story. Four stone "bridges" balustraded with carved openwork reach out to the corners of the room, connecting the platform with a gallery around the walls. Akbar is supposed to have sat enthroned on the platform, discussing affairs of state with his ministers seated in the galleries.

In the large Public Audience Chamber the emperor held audiences twice a day. The three Englishmen probably never had a chance to present to him their letters from the queen, but one of the three, who was a jeweler, was left "in service with the King . . . who did entertayne him verie well."

Ralph Fitch and his fellow merchant must have left Fathpur-Sikri disappointed at the failure of their mission, and within a few months Akbar himself had abandoned the city, taking with him his great household, courtiers, and government officials. The emperor never lived at Fathpur-Sikri again. The deserted palaces fell into decay, and after Akbar's death in 1605, his son Salim took up residence at Lahore in pomp and majesty as the Emperor Jahangir, the Conqueror of the World.

india and the great mughals—2

In 1615 an ambassador from England, Sir Thomas Roe, arrived at the court of the Emperor Jahangir to ask for trading privileges for English merchants. The ambassador brought handsome presents for the emperor, including a coach, a fine sword, and a virginal, a small keyboard instrument whose music delighted Jahangir. But Sir Thomas was ashamed of the dowdy appearance of his English dress, compared with the brilliant clothes of the Mughals. "Five years' allowance would not have furnished me with one indifferent suit sortable to theirs," he wrote sadly in his diary.

All about him at Jahangir's court, people were clad in the beautiful Indian silks and cottons which the merchants of England were so eager to buy. The men's coats and sashes and the women's saris were made of exquisite flower-patterned brocades, while cotton clothes were lavishly embroidered, printed with wood blocks or dyed in glowing colors. For the decoration of houses there were painted and printed cotton hangings and cushion covers with designs of musicians and dancers, singing birds and whole gardens of flowers and trees.

139

Above GARDEN SCENE
Detail from a dyed and painted cushion cover, Mughal, 1615–40
Right MUGHAL EMBROIDERY

The same lush tropical vegetation blossomed in the designs of the Mughal carpets. When the Emperor Humayun returned from exile in Persia, he brought with him Persian carpet weavers to teach the Indian craftsmen, but during the reign of Akbar the Indians began to break away from Persian models, as the miniature painters had done. Their rugs became incredibly fine and velvety in texture, with as many as a thousand knots to the square inch, and often portrayed landscapes with houses, animals and people. Flower designs grew larger, and carpets were bordered with naturalistic growing plants, which we also see in miniatures painted for Jahangir and his successor, Shah Jahan.

Jahangir was a keen naturalist. He employed artists to make careful studies of flowers and animals, and wherever he went he

SPOTTED FORKTAIL
Painting by Abu'l Hasan
Mughal, 1605–28

took painters to report on the chief events of his journeys, such as this exciting fight between two elephants. Watching battles between animals was a favorite sport of the Mughal emperors, and Jahangir rides his prancing horse in the foreground of the picture—a small figure but a recognizable portrait.

Dozens of portrait miniatures were painted of the emperor and his court. The figures were usually in profile; the bodies were modeled in the round, instead of following the linear style of the Persian artists, and in the faces the painters strove for an exact likeness, down to the last microscopic detail. Pictures of royal audiences were popular, and several painters would often collaborate on these group portraits. Jahangir was a keen critic of their work. "If any other person has put in the eye or eyebrow of the face," the emperor said, "I can perceive whose work the original face is, and who has painted the eye and eyebrow."

Jahangir was also a connoisseur of European paintings, particularly religious pictures, and his artists made such skillful copies of them that the English ambassador could not tell copies from originals. The emperor enjoyed discussing art with the ambassador, and considered Italian paintings superior to those sent from England.

By the time of Shah Jahan, who ascended the throne in 1628, Mughal painting had come a long way from the vigorous and fiery miniatures of Akbar's reign. Pictures had a static, almost architectural quality that reflected the immense wealth and power

141

of the court. In this splendid picture of the emperor, he rides his piebald horse in a flowery meadow with an empty background of blue-green sky. Around his neck hang ropes of pearls, large rubies, and emeralds; his belt and the sheath and hilt of his sword are of gold studded with jewels, and gold patterns adorn the red leather case of his short Turkish bow.

Though fine painters worked at his court, Shah Jahan's chief interest was in architecture. He himself designed the tomb of his beloved wife, and the building is still known by her title—Taj Mahal, the Crown of the Palace. The Taj is not an adventurous building; it sums up and brings to perfection ideas that were old and tried. More Persian than Indian in its design, it is a direct descendant of the tombs we have seen—the domed tomb at Tus and Timur's mausoleum at Samarkand, but while these are strong, massive, masculine buildings, the Taj is all feminine delicacy.

Shah Jahan chose a spacious site on the south bank of the river Jumna at Agra, and set the white marble tomb in a great Persian garden. He used to visit the tomb by water, arriving at the landing stage in his state barge, but the approach by road was even more beautiful, for the gardens were planned to lead up to the tomb. The long canal in which the building casts its shimmering white reflection reminds us of the reflecting pool in the garden of the Chehel Sotun at Isfahan. We may even think of the Court of the Pool in the Generalife at Granada on the far western edge of the old Arab Empire. There the long pool led us to a miniature palace; here it leads to the white marble mausoleum, as light and joyful in its design as a garden pavilion.

The tomb stands upon a marble platform like a stage, with minarets at the four corners, topped by the little cupolas we have seen at Fathpur-Sikri. Four larger domes of the same shape are set at the corners of the tomb itself, and between them is the main dome, purely Persian, its gently swelling shape rising from a high drum in matchless purity of line.

To the east and west of the tomb are two matching buildings, each topped by three domes and with small cupolas at the corners. The western building is a mosque; the eastern one, which balances it, is known as the *jawab*, or answer, and was used as a guesthouse for visitors to the tomb. Built of red sandstone with marble inlay about the entrance arches, the two structures make a brilliant contrast to the whiteness of the tomb, and complete the wonderful composition of architecture and garden.

Shah Jahan, who built the Taj and lies buried there beside his wife, was condemned to spend the last years of his life as a prisoner in his palace at Agra. He was imprisoned by his son Aurangzib, the World Shaker, who set out to gain control of the Mughal Empire in 1656 and fought a fierce war against his three brothers before he was secure upon the throne. Aurangzib reigned for fifty years, but he was a harsh, austere ruler and no patron of art. He concentrated on expanding his realm, which his successors were not strong enough to hold together.

Torn by civil wars and rebellions, the Mughal Empire collapsed in the eighteenth century, and in 1739 it was invaded by Nadir Shah, who had deposed the last Safavid ruler of Persia. He sacked Delhi and carried away to Persia the treasure of the Mughal emperors—untold quantities of gold and silver and gems and the fabulous Peacock Throne, entirely covered with jewels and enamels.

While the kingdoms of the Safavids and Mughals were crumbling into ruin, the Ottoman Sultan in Istanbul, the last powerful ruler left in the Moslem world, was walking in his tulip garden. Turkey was not swept by wars but by a craze for tulips, and Sultan Ahmed III, a man of peaceful tastes, was called the "Tulip Sultan." Leaving the government to his ministers, he fostered arts that were delicate, witty, and delightful. Life in Istanbul was gay with festivals and entertainments, and in the spring of the year the palace and city were filled with the joy of tulip time.

DETAIL OF
MUGHAL EMBROIDERY

the tulip sultan and the qajar shah

ON MOONLIT APRIL nights, in the reign of the Tulip Sultan, the gardens of the Seraglio Palace at Istanbul were aglow with lights and filled with moving throngs of people as brightly clad as the blossoming tulips. Graceful glass vases of tulips, interspersed with colored lamps, were arranged on tiers of shelves along the garden paths, and the air was musical with the singing of birds in golden cages.

Sultan Ahmed III was so fond of festivals that when his daughters were married or his sons entered school, the palace and the city would be given up to celebrations for days on end. The companies of tradesmen and craftsmen organized huge parades through the streets, as in the days of Suleyman the Magnificent. The festivities would go on long after dark, with fleets of pleasure boats on the Sea of Marmara, bearing musicians, dancers, and theatrical displays, which the sultan watched from a waterside garden house on Seraglio Point.

All these delights can be seen in the paintings of the court artist, Levni, whose masterpiece was a set of more than a hundred illustrations for a two-volume *Account of Festivities,* written by the Turkish poet Vehbi. His large pictures, often crowded with busy figures, are painted in light, bright colors. A two-page picture shows part of the procession of trades passing in review before the sultan, who watches from his throne under a red awning,

145

shaped like a domed Turkish tent. The tradesmen are escorted by
soldiers and a band of musicians. In the top left corner a bath
attendant is busily washing a customer's hair while they are
trundled along in a decorative wagon draped with towels. Below
them is a small covered stage on which a boy appears to be
making white candles; in the foreground at the bottom is a company of dancers, acrobats, and jesters, and ahead of them march

PROCESSION OF TRADESMEN
*Double-page illustration by
Levni from the Account of
Festivities, Turkish, early
18th century*

the serried ranks of the candlemakers, one of whom presents a
gift to a royal treasurer in a blue robe and immense turban.

Levni was the last famous Turkish miniature painter. In 1727,
during the reign of Ahmed III, the first printing press was set up
in Istanbul, and it became possible to print the Arabic script used
in Turkish books. This was to mean the end of hand-copied books
and painted illustrations. Istanbul was too close to Europe to be

unaffected by Western art, particularly with the European settlements of Pera and Galata just across the Golden Horn. It was not long before Turkish artists began to paint in oils and to imitate the European manner, and their work quickly lost its freshness.

We can see the European influence in architecture too, during the reign of Ahmed III. The Tulip Sultan and his court were less noted for the building of mosques than for garden pavilions and huge palaces where rooms were "wainscoted with mother-of-pearl, with emeralds like nails." An elegant small fountain built by the sultan outside the Imperial Gate of the Seraglio is typical of the taste of the time. There were many fountains in the streets of the city, provided by benefactors for the good of the people. Ahmed's fountain is a square building, its walls ornamented with inlaid marble and equipped with four drinking spouts and four outlets for drawing water, but its striking feature is the flaring roof and five little domes. The roof is not really in Turkish style at all but in the Chinese manner, which was so popular in France at that time and was brought back to Istanbul by the Turkish ambassador in Paris.

The arts of the potter and tilemaker, so brilliant in the sixteenth century, had long passed their prime by the eighteenth; but the Turks were still masters of many arts and crafts, which could be seen in the covered streets and cavelike shops of the Istanbul bazaar. "Every trade has its distinct alley," wrote an

SULTAN AHMED
FOUNTAIN,
ISTANBUL

PRAYER CARPET
Kula, 18th century

LADY WITH A VEIL
*From a painting
by Levni*

English sightseer in 1718. "The *bésisten*, or jewellers' quarter, shews so much riches, such a vast quantity of diamonds, and all kind of precious stones, that they dazzle the sight. The embroiderers' also is very glittering, and people walk here as much for diversion as business." But to European visitors the best known Turkish craft was carpet making. Many travelers found their way to the carpet bazaar and sat with the merchants over tiny cups of sweet black coffee, bargaining by the hour for beautiful carpets from Anatolia or the Caucasus.

Each town where carpets were made had its own peculiar patterns. In the eighteenth century the weavers of Kula and Ghiordes in Anatolia produced fine prayer carpets with the traditional design of the prayer niche, or *mihrab*. In the Kula rugs the *mihrab* might be filled with a landscape, a repeating pattern of houses and trees. The weavers of Kula also made splendid garden carpets like those made in northwestern Persia, just over the Turkish border. These carpets took their design from the plan of a typical Persian garden. Light-colored bands with a pattern of wavy lines represented water channels and divided the field into four, or eight, symmetrical plots, planted with stiff little trees and flowers.

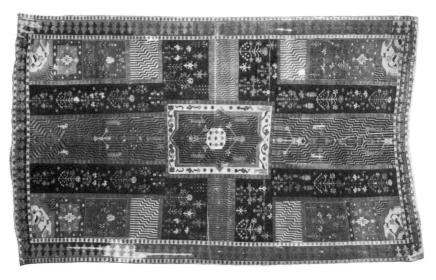

GARDEN CARPET, *Persian, 18th century*

Carpet weaving in Persia in the eighteenth and nineteenth centuries was no longer the glorious art of Safavid times, which had produced such masterpieces as the Ardebil carpet and the silken rugs of the court. All arts had declined in Persia during the terrible period of strife and confusion that had followed the fall of the Safavid dynasty, but Fath Ali Shah, who reigned from 1797 to 1834, was determined to bring about an artistic revival. He was the second of a new dynasty, the Qajars, who were to rule Persia throughout the nineteenth century and had chosen as their capital the brown, mud-walled city of Tehran, on the old trade route between Tabriz and Samarkand.

No great masterpieces were produced in Persia at this time, but craftsmen excelled in the making of small exquisite things. Isfahan was still a center of crafts, as it had been for hundreds of years. The streets of the bazaar were loud with the clang of the coppersmiths' hammers, beating out trays and household pots. Nearby the *chink-chink* of small hammers could be heard from the silversmiths' shops where tiny delicate designs were engraved on silver vases. Fine floral carpets were made there, and the shops were gay with *kalamkar,* the beautiful cotton hangings and draperies with printed patterns in many colors.

DETAIL OF
KALAMKAR DESIGN

150

Shiraz, the city of roses, was famous for flower painting in the nineteenth century. Pictures of lush, naturalistic flowers were bound into albums, and gardens of roses blossomed on book covers, pen cases, and powder boxes, made of papier-mâché. Even pottery was painted with flowers and scenic views, though seldom with very happy results.

The painting of miniatures for manuscripts, especially copies of the *Shah Nama*, continued well into the nineteenth century, and minor artists carried on, a little crudely, the old conventions of the miniature painters of the past.

The Western style of painting had been introduced into Persia in the seventeenth century by a Persian artist who traveled in Italy. From that time on, the Western influence began to appear in the work of Persian painters, and in the time of Fath Ali Shah they took to painting large pictures on canvas. We find some elegant oils showing the shah with his long black beard, but as a whole, Persian and Western styles did not make a good mixture.

MINIATURE PAINTING
*From a Shah Nama
manuscript
Persian, 19th century*

Throughout the lands that had belonged to the old Arab Empire the story was the same. Western styles of art, Western goods, and Western ideas were spreading over the Near East and into India at a time when Moslem art was weak and lacking the fire and inspiration of the past. If we look back over the story of Moslem art, we shall see that its most splendid periods were in the times of prosperity under great rulers. These men might be despots, cruel and ruthless, but it was they who could afford and demand the best in art. They built the palaces and the largest mosques, the noble tombs and public buildings. Artists and craftsmen under their protection were spurred to do the finest work, and to experiment and improve on what had been done before.

But the age of these powerful rulers belonged to the past. The old kingdoms were breaking up, and in a time of unrest and change Moslem art declined, followed old, lifeless patterns, and could not compete with the vigor of Western ideas.

By the beginning of the twentieth century, most cities of the Moslem world were no longer remote, mysterious places known only to a few adventurers from the West, and everywhere the years of contact with Europeans were to have their effect on Moslem art and architecture. Nowhere is this more clearly shown than in Tehran, the capital of modern Iran. If we visit Tehran today, we see a city that Fath Ali Shah and his people would hardly recognize. Here and there they would pick out a few familiar landmarks, including the shah's Gulistan Palace, in all the glory of its painted tiles and mirror-covered rooms; but they would find few traces of the sleepy mud-walled town they knew, where caravans of camels padded through the dusty streets, bound for Tabriz or Samarkand.

DESIGN FROM A
GLAZED TILE
Persian, 19th century

the old and the new

TODAY ONE OF the main squares of Tehran is dominated by a bronze statue of the poet Firdausi, the author of the *Shah Nama*. He stands as though reciting the verses of his great epic, still known and loved in Iran. At the foot of his high white pedestal is a lawn with pools and fountains, and in the distance behind him are the bare brown foothills and snow-capped ridges of the Elburz Mountains. Traffic swirls around the edge of the garden; traffic lights flicker red and green; and along the wide avenues that converge on the square rise new buildings of glass and concrete that might be office blocks in London or New York.

A stone's throw away from the statue, down the broad avenue that bears the poet's name, we can see ancient arts and crafts whose origins are lost in history. We tread on carpets spread out on the pavement for the sun to mellow their colors, and watch the carpet weavers at work within, seated before the upright loom, tying the woolen knots to the strong threads of the warp.

Farther down the street we come to shops stocked with crafts from all parts of the country. There are marquetry boxes from

153

WOODBLOCK FOR
PRINTING KALAMKAR
Isfahan, 20th century

Shiraz and tribal carpets and bags made by the nomad people of the west and south. From Meshed come black stone vases and plates engraved with flowers, birds, and animals, and turquoise jewelry set with stones from the ancient mines of Nishapur; and among the many arts of Isfahan—the printed cottons and the metalwork of copper and silver—are scores of dainty miniatures in the style of the seventeenth century, showing the hunting scenes, gardens, and palaces painted by the artists of old.

Then, when it seems as though all painting is an imitation of the past, we find artists who have broken away completely from the miniature tradition. In oils and large free watercolors they paint landscapes of the Elburz Mountains or the Caspian shore, studies of animals, and vivid portraits of the people of Iran—a wise old dervish, a camel driver, or a proud tribesman. Like other modern artists of the Near East, these painters work in a realistic Western style; but in the Moslem art of the past the artists of today have a noble tradition of abstract design on which to build, and some painters are drawing new inspiration from ancient decorative themes—the arabesque in all its variety and the beautiful flowing shapes of Arabic script.

Old patterns live on in the designs of carpets, too, and the carpet remains the best-loved form of art in Iran, both a delight to the eye and a necessity of life. A bright new office building in Tehran is furnished with modern tribal rugs, and no Iranian home, new or old, is complete without carpets. The carpets make the home. They not only cover the floors of the house, filling the rooms with all the color of a springtime garden; they are spread on the grass outdoors for people to sit on, just as we have seen in the old miniatures.

MOSAIC TILES
Isfahan, 20th century

CONTEMPORARY
IRANIAN PAINTING:
Left TWO DEER *by Afsary*
Above DERVISH *by Chitsaz*

Persian gardens, like those that inspired the painters and carpet designers of the past, can be found in the middle of Tehran, hidden behind the high brown walls along the side streets. Even in the terminal building at the airport there is a little garden with green plants and running water, as though to welcome travelers arriving weary from the desert.

The noisy coming and going of airplanes has replaced the plodding camel caravans of bygone travelers, but the desert, with its old caravan roads and nomad encampments of black tents, lies within sight of the airfield. When we climb aboard an airplane and fly westward from Tehran, we enter a world well known to the travelers of the past, a world that is older than Islam and the beginnings of Moslem art. The sprawling modern city is left behind, and below us and all around us, as far as the foothills of the Elburz Mountains, is the brown desert, part of the great belt of dry country that stretches almost from Spain to India.

Across this harsh bare earth, where the airplane casts its moving shadow, rode the Arab conquerors of thirteen centuries ago.

155

After their whirlwind conquest and the founding of their empire, the desert was the pathway for new invaders, sweeping into the Arab lands from the East. They came to conquer and destroy, and remained to enrich and beautify the ravaged cities. And always there were the merchants, carrying their goods along the desert trade routes, and with their caravans went pilgrims and scholars and artists, bearers of new ideas to the far corners of the empire.

From the early days of Islam, the Moslems were great travelers, as we have seen. Down through the centuries we have journeyed, as they did, to the cities of the Moslem world, starting out from Damascus, the capital of the Umayyad caliphs, who loved the desert so well they could not bear to be pent up in their city, beautiful though it was.

Soon we shall see Damascus again. We are passing over Baghdad, a brown city clustered around a brown river. Now we fly west along the old route of the caravans, and Baghdad slips away behind us, lost in the vastness of the desert. So many cities of the old Arab Empire were surrounded by desert, with houses and mosques and palaces huddled together beside a river or an oasis. In these cities, the desert was the unchanging background of people's lives, and played its own role in shaping their art.

As we look down on the barren earth far below, we can understand how its bare brownness made men love color, especially the brilliant cloudless blue of the sky. Did the desert also give them their love of rich patterns? Perhaps it was the stark featureless horizon of their world, and the vast distances in which they felt so small, that inspired the Moslem artists to compose designs so miniature and so complicated—patterns that took many days to make and many hours for the eye of the beholder to follow the twists and turns of the arabesques.

But most important of all to the desert people, and to those who traveled the long caravan roads, were the heat and dust and fierce sunlight of the waterless land. Green trees, cool shade, and running water were more precious to them than gold, and Paradise itself became a garden.

High in the airplane we have felt none of the torture of the desert marches. We know nothing of the three weeks of cruel traveling that brought the caravans from Baghdad to Damascus, with the winding lines of camels and donkeys and the men tramping beside them, gaunt and sun-scorched in the furnace heat. Yet even to us it is good to see the spread of dark green trees at the foot of the mountains. No wonder the Prophet Muhammad considered Damascus to be a Paradise on earth!

Now we are over the city of the Umayyad caliphs, ringed around with the wonderful green orchards, watered by the Barada River coming down from the mountains through its narrow valley. In the center of the town we see the Great Mosque, laid out below us like a plan. The simple outlines of its courtyard and prayer hall go back to the small humble buildings in Arabia where Muhammad and his few followers gathered together for the worship of Allah, and where men repeated the creed that was to become a battle cry ringing across the world: "There is no God but Allah, and Muhammad is his Prophet."

We have traveled from end to end of the empire conquered by the followers of Muhammad. As the airplane lifts over the mountains and Damascus fades into the distance, our journey is nearly over, but the story we have followed in this book has no ending. It goes on wherever artists and craftsmen are at work in the countries of the Moslem world; and as the arts of Islam were enriched by fresh ideas in the past, so in the days to come, with the blending of old and new, another exciting chapter will be added to the story of Moslem art.

illustration sources

FRONTISPIECE: A ruler gives audience. Miniature by Farhad from KHAVARAN NAMA, Shiraz, *c.* 1480. (Metropolitan Museum of Art, Rogers Fund, 1955)

PAGE

Drawings